Psychology: an Introduction

STUDY GUIDE

Nicky Hayes
and Paula Topley

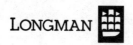
LONGMAN

Longman Group Limited
Longman House, Burnt Mill, Harlow,
Essex CM20 2JE, England
and Associated Companies throughout the world.

© Longman Group Limited 1995

First published 1995

ISBN 0 582 24613 X

Designed, typeset and illustrated by Stephen I Pargeter, Banbury
Set in 11/14 Times

Produced by Longman Singapore Publishers Pte Ltd
Printed in Singapore

It is the publisher's policy to use paper manufactured from sustainable forests.

Acknowledgements

We are indebted to the following for permission to reproduce copyright material:

The Association for the Teaching of Psychology, c/o The British Psychological Society, St. Andrew's House, 48 Princess Road East, Leicester, LE1 7DR for 'Ethics in Psychological Research: Guidelines for students at Pre-degree Levels'; The British Psychological Society for the article 'Revised Ethical Principles for Conducting Research with Human Participants' from *The Psychologist* (1990) 3(6), 270-272.

We are also indebted to the *Midland Examining Group* and the *Northern Examinations and Assessment Board* for permission to reproduce past examination questions.

Contents

Introduction

This book is designed to be used hand in hand with *Psychology: an Introduction*. It is a workbook which will build up your study and exam skills as well as your knowledge of psychology. By working through this book, you will find that learning becomes easier, and that tests and exams become more manageable.

Each chapter consists of a self-contained set of exercises which will help you to build up your knowledge of psychology. The chapters of the Guide link with the chapters in *Psychology: an Introduction*, by Nicky Hayes and Sue Orrell. They have the same chapter numbers, and refer to the same information, so you will need to have a copy of *Psychology: an Introduction* to hand while you are working through the *Study Guide*.

The exercises in each chapter are also designed to build up your study and exam skills. A large part of taking exams successfully is the result of practice. By working through the activities in this book, you will gain lots of practice in dealing with questions in an intelligent way. (If you would like some advice on how to tackle your GCSE exam and how to revise effectively, look at *The GCSE Survival Guide* by Nicky Hayes, which is also published by Longman.)

How to use your *Study Guide*

1   First, open your copy of *Psychology: an Introduction* and your copy of the *Study Guide* so that they are both at the start of the chapter you are working on. Begin by reading through the chapter in *Psychology: an Introduction*, and think about the general points that it raises. Don't worry too much about memorising specific details at this stage. Instead, tackle the essay plans in the *Study Guide*, which deal with taking an overview of the topic, and looking at some of the general issues and debates concerned in it.

Incidentally, not many GCSE exams actually require you to write essays nowadays, so we don't actually ask you to write the essays themselves – although if you should choose to do so it would help you to develop fluency when explaining psychological ideas. What we ask you to do here is to plan your essays – to work out what you would put into an essay if you had to write one under exam conditions. Doing this gives you practice in identifying relevant knowledge and using it to develop an argument. It is even better if you can compare your essay plans with a friend who is doing the same course.

2   When you have done the essay plans, try the 'key chunks'. Taking each one in turn, begin by reading through that section of the chapter in *Psychology: an Introduction*. Then use the chart provided in the *Study Guide* to make notes about the methods of study, criticisms or evaluative points, and any ethical issues that arise. Read the next section of the chapter and fill in the chart for that one too. Carry on doing this until you have worked through each of the chunks in turn.

3   When you have completed the chart, begin writing your mark schemes. There are seven short-answer questions for each chapter in the *Study Guide*, and two of them have mark schemes already written. Have a look at these and see how the 10 marks for each question have been divided up. Then draft a set of mark schemes for each of the other five questions. If you need some extra help with this, you can look at the mark schemes in the other chapters.

4   When you have completed all of the mark schemes, go back to the first question and read about it in *Psychology: an Introduction*. Then, without looking at the mark scheme, try answering the question using the space provided in the *Study Guide*. (If you really want a challenge, you could leave this for a day or two until you have forgotten the mark

scheme, but that's up to you.) Give yourself 10 minutes to answer each question. When you've finished all the questions, go back to the mark schemes and the chapter and see what marks your answer would have earned.

5   Now turn to the practical work exercise and fill in the items that you need to identify for the study. Even though you will only need to do a couple of studies in full for your GCSE coursework, you do need to be able to identify things like independent and dependent variables, so this is a useful exercise. It will also help you to choose which practicals you would like to carry out for your own GCSE exam. If the study in the chapter you are doing is one that you are going to carry out fully, use the guidelines in the Appendix to help you to prepare your report.

6   Now try the real exam question under exam conditions. Clear everything off your desk except for pens and paper, time yourself carefully, and answer the question as quickly as you can. You could give yourself a fixed amount of time for this (about 20 minutes to half an hour), or you could simply do it as fast as possible, and aim to get quicker as you do each chapter.

7   Finally, see how well you do on the chapter quiz. The answers are in the Appendix so you can mark your own work quite easily.

We hope that you will find it enjoyable to work through the different exercises in the *Study Guide*. We know that doing this will help you to learn. Each of these exercises has been thoroughly tested by psychology students throughout our many years of teaching, and we are confident that they will help you to understand your work better and to be more successful in your exams.

Nicky Hayes and Paula Topley

Chapter 1 – the process of maturation

This chapter can be divided into four major segments, as follows:

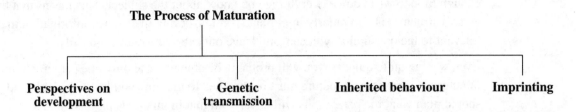

The Process of Maturation

- **Perspectives on development**
- **Genetic transmission**
- **Inherited behaviour**
- **Imprinting**

Each of those segments can then be subdivided into smaller tree diagrams. These can be useful in helping you to structure your revision.

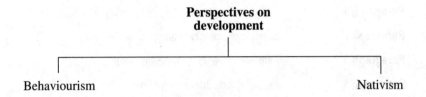

Perspectives on development

- Behaviourism
- Nativism

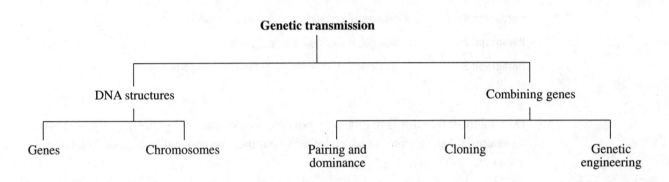

Genetic transmission

- DNA structures
  - Genes
  - Chromosomes
- Combining genes
  - Pairing and dominance
  - Cloning
  - Genetic engineering

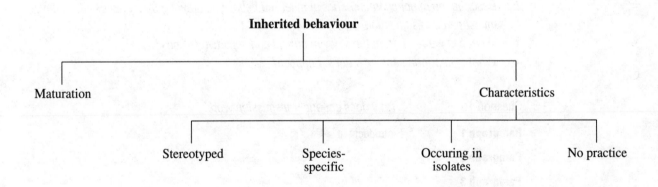

Inherited behaviour

- Maturation
- Characteristics
  - Stereotyped
  - Species-specific
  - Occuring in isolates
  - No practice

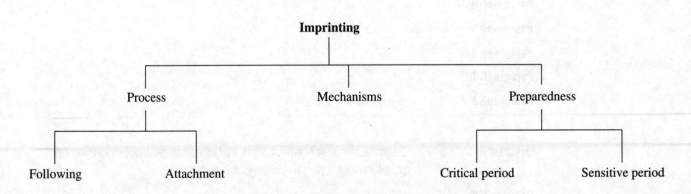

Imprinting

- Process
  - Following
  - Attachment
- Mechanisms
- Preparedness
  - Critical period
  - Sensitive period

Planning an essay

When you are planning an essay for an examination, remember that you won't have enough time to write down everything you know about the subject. This means that the essay's structure is particularly important. You must bring in as much information that is relevant to the question as you can, and leave out extra or irrelevant details.

Even writing quite quickly, you will probably be able to write only one paragraph in five minutes, so your essay structure must be matched to the time you have available and you should plan what the paragraphs will cover with that in mind. Using this method, a 45-minute essay involves five minutes' thinking time and produces eight paragraphs. For example:

Outline the roles played by <u>both</u> genetic inheritance <u>and</u> the environment in human development.

Paragraph 1	introduction: inheritance and learning
Paragraph 2	description: genotype and phenotype
Paragraph 3	inherited behaviour/predispositions
Paragraph 4	example, e.g., infant sociability
Paragraph 5	description: conditioning and imitation
Paragraph 6	example of conditioning, e.g., avoiding pain
Paragraph 7	example of imitation, e.g., social roles
Paragraph 8	conclusion: learning and inheritance both important

Do remember that this is not the only possible way of answering this question – it is only an example. Now try producing some essay outlines for yourself, using the following questions:

1 *How does genetic transmission work?*
2 *Describe the major characteristics of inherited behaviour, drawing from studies which have investigated this question.*
3 *What can we learn from the study of critical and sensitive periods?*
4 *What is imprinting and how does it happen?*

Question 1:	*How does genetic transmission work?*
Paragraph 1	introduction:
Paragraph 2	
Paragraph 3	
Paragraph 4	
Paragraph 5	
Paragraph 6	
Paragraph 7	
Paragraph 8	conclusion:

Question 2:	*Describe the major characteristics of inherited behaviour, drawing from studies which have investigated this question.*
Paragraph 1	introduction:
Paragraph 2	

Paragraph 3

Paragraph 4

Paragraph 5

Paragraph 6

Paragraph 7

Paragraph 8   conclusion:

Question 3:   *What can we learn from the study of critical and sensitive periods?*

Paragraph 1   introduction:

Paragraph 2

Paragraph 3

Paragraph 4

Paragraph 5

Paragraph 6

Paragraph 7

Paragraph 8   conclusion:

Question 4:   *What is imprinting and how does it happen?*

Paragraph 1   introduction:

Paragraph 2

Paragraph 3

Paragraph 4

Paragraph 5

Paragraph 6

Paragraph 7

Paragraph 8   conclusion:

Chapter summary

(*Psychology: an Introduction*, page 14)

1   Traditionally there has been a distinction in psychology between those who believe that development is mainly inherited and those who believe that it is mainly learned.

2   Through the process of genetic transmission we inherit half of our genes and chromosomes from each of our parents.

3   Each gene is responsible for a particular item of development which will occur when the organism is at the right stage of maturity.

4   Inherited behaviour takes the form of fixed action sequences, which are triggered off by specific stimuli.

5   The process of imprinting shows one method by which genetic mechanisms and environmental stimuli interact.

6   Imprinting and many other aspects of development occur during a sensitive period when the organism is particularly ready for the right environmental stimuli.

Key sections for revision

1   nativists and empiricists
2   genetic transmission
3   genes and development
4   fixed action patterns
5   imprinting
6   sensitive periods

Issues and perspectives

Using the following table, note down any features of interest which relate to the key sections of the chapter.

Key section	Methods of study	Evaluation and/or criticism	Ethical issues
1 nativists and empiricists			
2 genetic transmission			
3 genes and development			
4 fixed action patterns			
5 imprinting			
6 sensitive periods			

Revision questions

Short-answer questions are useful for testing your knowledge of an area while you are revising, and for making sure that you understand it. They also often appear in examinations, and when they do you will have only a limited amount of time to answer them. The questions will be marked according to the information you have used to answer them and what you can attain marks for will be set out in a mark scheme.

Here are two 10-mark questions, with typical marking schemes which an examiner might use to assess answers.

Briefly describe the two major schools of thought in the nature/nurture debate.

correct naming	(up to)	2 marks
description of empiricist school	(up to)	4 marks
description of nativist school	(up to)	4 marks
		Total 10 marks

What are the main characteristics of inherited behaviour described by Lorenz?

definition: innate behaviour	(up to)	2 marks
stereotypes	(up to)	2 marks
species-specific	(up to)	2 marks
shown in isolates	(up to)	2 marks
doesn't need practice	(up to)	2 marks
		Total 10 marks

As you can see, each question has its own mark scheme and these share out the marks between the different types of knowledge needed to answer the question.

Bearing this in mind, try to work out your own mark schemes for each of the following questions. Each question is worth 10 marks. If you feel that you need more help, look at the mark schemes in the other chapters.

1   *How is genetic information transmitted from parents to child?*

2   *Briefly describe what is meant by cloning <u>and</u> genetic engineering.*

3   *Give an example of inherited behaviour and describe the mechanisms involved in its production.*

4   *Describe the main features of imprinting.*

5   *Distinguish between a sensitive and a critical period in development.*

When you have written each mark scheme, turn to the relevant pages in your textbook and make sure that your scheme reflects the information covered by that topic.

Answering revision questions

Now try answering each of these questions, giving yourself 15 minutes to complete each one. At the end of that time, mark your answer, using the mark scheme that you have developed.

(NB: It is essential that you write the mark scheme <u>before</u> you try to answer the question! Doing it the other way round would be completely pointless because you would be too influenced by what you have already written.)

12

1 *How is genetic information transmitted from parents to child?*

2 *Briefly describe what is meant by cloning <u>and</u> genetic engineering.*

3 *Give an example of inherited behaviour and describe the mechanisms involved in its production.*

4 *Describe the main features of imprinting.*

5 *Distinguish between a sensitive and a critical period in development.*

A suggestion for practical work

Use Example 1.2 on pages 9–10 of *Psychology: an Introduction*. This is an observational study, looking at differences in how people interpret animal behaviour.

In this study, you can ask two people to perform the same task (recording the behaviour of an animal) and compare what they produce. Sort their statements using the categories of behavioural descriptions/intentional descriptions/anthropomorphic descriptions of the behaviour, and compare them.

Carrying out the study

You will need to identify the following (see Chapter 22, pages 424–8 of *Psychology: an Introduction*):

hypothesis _____

null hypothesis _____

variable 1 _____

variable 2 _____

controls. _____

ethical considerations _____

_____

_____

_____

_____

Make notes on how you will carry out this research. _____

_____

_____

_____

_____

Analysing the results

First, present your results in a table. Use the three categories as your columns, and the first and second observer for your rows. You can find instructions for drawing up a table in Appendix 2A (page 205).

You will also need a bar chart to display your results visually. In a formal report, this should be done on graph paper. Graphs, bar charts, pie charts, etc. are all called figures and they all need a title saying exactly what the figure is showing. You can find instructions on how to draw a bar chart in Appendix 2B (page 205).

Reporting the study

You are now ready to write up your study using the correct format. Use Checklist B, in Appendix 3 (page 210), to make sure you have included everything you need.

Sample examination questions

Midlands Examining Group, February 1989, Paper reference: 682
Comparative Module, Source B, Questions 6/7

Flying a kite

Farmer Seth: 'I see you be using a new way to keep the birds off your field.'

Farmer Dan: 'That be right boy, I put my scarecrow in the barn, he be no use at all. He don't frighten them birds no more.'

Farmer Seth: 'What will you be using now then?'

Farmer Dan: 'I be using a kite.'

Farmer Seth: 'A kite! You daft old fool, that'll never work. I'll stick to my scarecrow. He's done me well for twenty years now.'

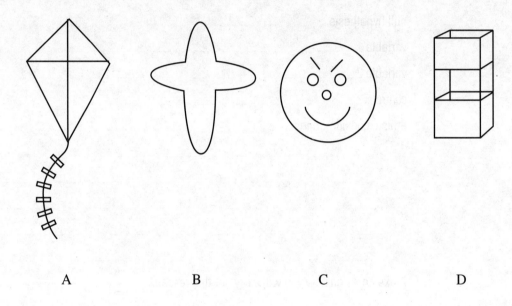

A   B   C   D

 QUESTIONS

6   (a)   Which kite was most likely to scare the birds away?

_____ [1]

(b)   Give reasons for your answer.

_____

_____

_____

_____ [3]

7   Describe another example from psychology where a simple shaped model has been used to affect the behaviour of an animal.

_____

_____

_____

_____

_____ [4]

Chapter quiz

Answer the following questions in no longer than 10 minutes:

1   How many pairs of chromosomes do human beings have?

2   What name is given to a gene which does not influence the phenotype because its matching partner is more influential?

3   What did Hebb use as an example of the inseparable link between environment and heredity?

4   What is the main characteristic of animals which show evidence of imprinting?

5   What feature of the belly of a male stickleback triggers attack behaviour in other males?

6   In what way are all the kiwi fruit on the market related to one another?

7   What did the behaviourist school believe was the main cause of development?

8   What name is give to a time when a certain form of learning must happen or else it never will.

9   What process involves taking a segment of DNA from a chromosome and replacing it with another segment?

10   What do we call behaviour which is the same each time and never varies?

Chapter 2 – Forms of learning

This chapter can be divided into two major segments, as follows:

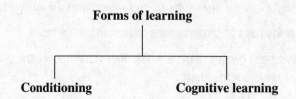

Each of those segments can then be subdivided into smaller tree diagrams. These can be useful in helping you to structure your revision.

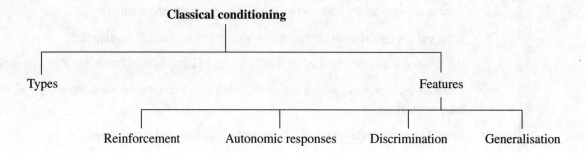

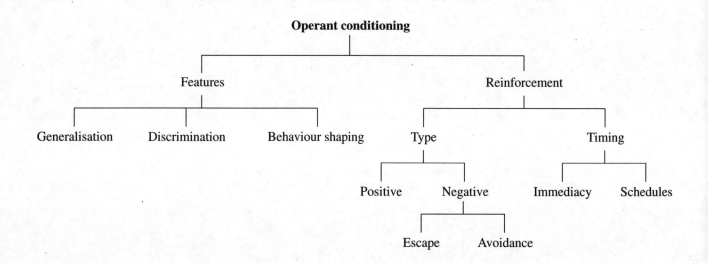

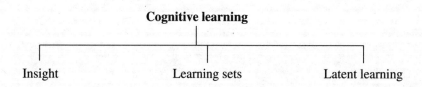

Planning an essay

When you are planning an essay for an examination, remember that you won't have enough time to write down everything you know about the subject. This means that the essay's structure is particularly important. You must bring in as much information that is relevant to the question as you can, and leave out extra or irrelevant details.

Even writing quite quickly, you will probably be able to write only one paragraph in five minutes, so your essay structure must be matched to the time you have available and you should plan what the paragraphs will cover with that in mind. Using this method, a 45-minute essay involves five minutes' thinking time and produces eight paragraphs. For example:

SAMPLE QUESTION

Discuss the role of reinforcement in learning.

Paragraph 1	introduction: reinforcement as strengthening learning
Paragraph 2	classical conditioning: reinforcement as exercise
Paragraph 3	operant conditioning: positive and negative reinforcement
Paragraph 4	classical example: e.g., exam fear/desensitisation
Paragraph 5	partial reinforcement, e.g., gambling
Paragraph 6	shaping behaviour, secondary and immediate, e.g., autistic children, tokens
Paragraph 7	non-reinforced learning, e.g., latent learning, imitation
Paragraph 8	conclusion: reinforcement is a powerful influence but not everything

Do remember that this is not the only possible way of answering this question: it is only an example. Now try producing some essay outlines for yourself, using the following questions:

QUESTIONS

1   *How may classical conditioning affect human behaviour?*
2   *'It is better to reinforce correct behaviour than to punish inappropriate action'. How may correct behaviour be reinforced?*
3   *'All human behaviour can be explained in terms of the principles of conditioning.' Do you agree? Give reasons for your answer.*
4   *What alternative forms of learning, other than conditioning, have psychologists investigated?*

Question 1:	*How may classical conditioning affect human behaviour?*
Paragraph 1	introduction:
Paragraph 2	
Paragraph 3	
Paragraph 4	
Paragraph 5	
Paragraph 6	
Paragraph 7	
Paragraph 8	conclusion:

Question 2:	*'It is better to reinforce correct behaviour than to punish inappropriate action'. How may correct behaviour be reinforced?*
Paragraph 1	introduction:
Paragraph 2	
Paragraph 3	

Paragraph 4

Paragraph 5

Paragraph 6

Paragraph 7

Paragraph 8   conclusion:

Question 3:   *'All human behaviour can be explained in terms of the principles of conditioning.' Do you agree? Give reasons for your answer.*

Paragraph 1   introduction:

Paragraph 2

Paragraph 3

Paragraph 4

Paragraph 5

Paragraph 6

Paragraph 7

Paragraph 8   conclusion:

Question 4:   *What alternative forms of learning, other than conditioning, have psychologists investigated?*

Paragraph 1   introduction:

Paragraph 2

Paragraph 3

Paragraph 4

Paragraph 5

Paragraph 6

Paragraph 7

Paragraph 8   conclusion:

Chapter summary

(*Psychology: an Introduction*, page 29)

1   One-trial learning is a very basic form of learning. It involves a rapidly formed association between a stimulus and a response.
2   Pavlov investigated the process of classical conditioning, in which involuntary responses can be produced to a learned stimulus.
3   Presentation of the stimulus in classical conditioning may vary. The three main methods are: trace conditioning, simultaneous conditioning, and delayed conditioning.
4   Operant conditioning is the conditioning of voluntary behaviour through positive or negative reinforcement.
5   Operant conditioning can be used to create novel forms of behaviour, through the process of behaviour-shaping
6   Reinforcement schedules may produce very strong forms of learning, and different kinds of reinforcements may have different effects.
7   Insight learning and latent learning are both cognitive forms of learning, which cannot be explained purely in behaviourist terms.

Key sections for revision

1 one-trial learning
2 classical conditioning
3 stimulus presentation
4 operant conditioning
5 behaviour shaping
6 reinforcement schedules
7 cognitive learning

Issues and perspectives

Using the following table, note down any features of interest which relate to the key sections of the chapter.

Key section	Methods of study	Evaluation and criticism	Ethical issues
1 one-trial learning			
2 classical conditioning			
3 stimulus presentation			
4 operant conditioning			
5 behaviour shaping			
6 reinforcement schedules			
7 cognitive learning			

Revision questions

Short-answer questions are useful for testing your knowledge of an area while you are revising, and for making sure that you understand it. They also often appear in examinations, and when they do you will have only a limited amount of time to answer them. The questions will be marked according to the information you have used to answer them and what you can attain marks for will be set out in a mark scheme.

Here are two 10-mark questions, with typical marking schemes which an examiner might use to assess answers.

Using a specific example, describe the three stages of classical conditioning.

definition of classical conditioning		1 mark
before conditioning (US, UR, etc.)	(up to)	2 marks
during conditioning	(up to)	2 marks
after conditioning	(up to)	2 marks
appropriate use of example	(up to)	3 marks
		Total 10 marks

Describe Menzies's study of classical conditioning.

description of study	(up to)	3 marks
identification of CS, US, etc.	(up to)	3 marks
outcome of study		1 mark
implications of study	(up to)	2 marks
		Total 10 marks

As you can see, each question has its own mark scheme and these share out the marks between the different types of knowledge needed to answer the question.

Bearing this in mind, try to work out your own mark schemes for each of the following questions. Each question is worth 10 marks. If you feel that you need more help, look at the mark schemes in the other chapters.

1   *What is one-trial learning?*

2   *Outline the main principles of operant conditioning.*

3   *Describe the five main types of reinforcement schedules and their effects.*

4   *How might you use operant conditioning to train a mouse to salivate when it presses a lever?*

5   *Outline two types of learning which are not based on behavioural reinforcement.*

When you have written your mark scheme, turn to the relevant pages in your textbook and make sure that your scheme reflects the information covered by that topic.

Answering revision questions

Now try answering each of these questions, giving yourself 15 minutes to complete each one. At the end of that time, mark your answer, using the mark scheme that you have developed.

(NB: It is essential that you write the mark scheme <u>before</u> you try to answer the question! Doing it the other way round would be completely pointless because you would be too influenced by what you have already written.)

 **QUESTIONS**

1   *What is one-trial learning?*

2   *Outline the main principles of operant conditioning.*

3   *Describe the five main types of reinforcement schedules and their effects.*

4   *How might you use operant conditioning to train a mouse to salivate when it presses a lever?*

5   *Outline two types of learning which are not based on behavioural reinforcement.*

A suggestion for practical work

Use Example 2.1 on page 25 of *Psychology: an Introduction*. This experiment allows you to investigate reinforcement in everyday life.

You will need to establish an experimental group which receives reinforcement, and a control group which has the same task but without the reinforcement.

Carrying out the study

In planning your study, you will need to identify the following (consult Chapter 22, pages 424–8 of *Psychology: an Introduction* if you need further explanation):

hypothesis _____

null hypothesis _____

independent variable _____

dependent variable _____

design _____

controls _____

ethical considerations _____

_____

_____

_____

_____

Make notes on how you will carry out this research. _____

_____

_____

_____

_____

Analysing the results

You will need a summary table of results which includes the mean, median and mode for your two groups. It should be called Table 1 and will need a title telling your reader exactly what it is about. Use the instructions in Appendix 2A (page 205) to draw up your table.

You will also need a diagram to display your findings visually. For this, you will need to use a bar chart. One of the bars will represent the scores when people were reinforced, and the other will represent the scores when they were not. This will be called Fig. 1. Use the instructions in Appendix 2B (page 205) to draw up a bar chart for your results.

Reporting the study

You are now ready to write up your study using the correct format. Use Checklist A, in Appendix 3 (page 210), to make sure you have included everything you need.

Sample examination questions

Northern Examining Association, June 1990
Paper 2, Question 5
Paper reference: 2175

Malcolm the rat was taught a long sequence of behaviours.

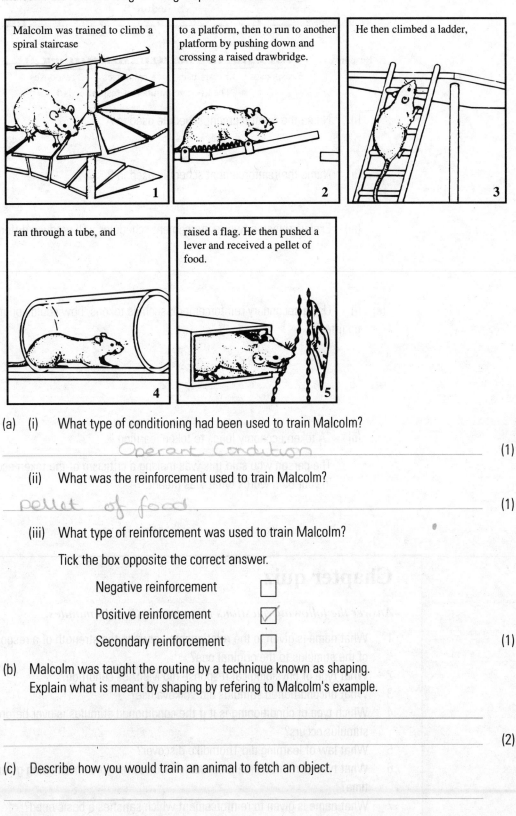

Malcolm was trained to climb a spiral staircase

to a platform, then to run to another platform by pushing down and crossing a raised drawbridge.

He then climbed a ladder,

ran through a tube, and

raised a flag. He then pushed a lever and received a pellet of food.

(a) (i) What type of conditioning had been used to train Malcolm?

Operant Condition (1)

(ii) What was the reinforcement used to train Malcolm?

pellet of food (1)

(iii) What type of reinforcement was used to train Malcolm?

Tick the box opposite the correct answer.

Negative reinforcement ☐

Positive reinforcement ☑

Secondary reinforcement ☐ (1)

(b) Malcolm was taught the routine by a technique known as shaping.
Explain what is meant by shaping by refering to Malcolm's example.

(2)

(c) Describe how you would train an animal to fetch an object.

(3)

(d)   The diagram below shows two reinforcement schedules A and B.

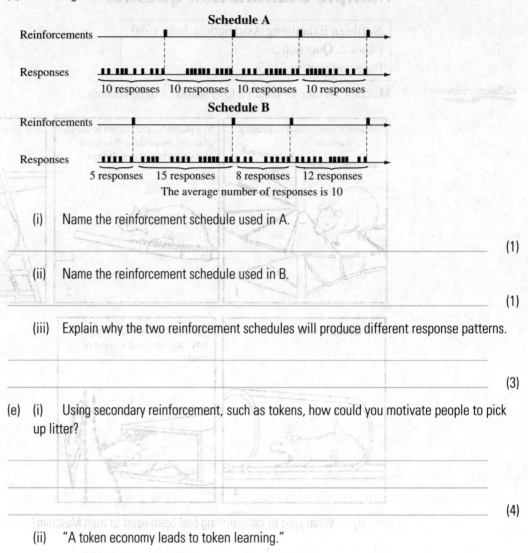

Schedule A

Reinforcements ⎯⎯⎯⎯⎯⎯⎯⎯⎯⎯⎯⎯⎯⎯⎯⎯⎯⎯⎯⎯⎯⎯⎯⎯⎯⎯

Responses

10 responses   10 responses   10 responses   10 responses

Schedule B

Reinforcements ⎯⎯⎯⎯⎯⎯⎯⎯⎯⎯⎯⎯⎯⎯⎯⎯⎯⎯⎯⎯⎯⎯⎯⎯⎯⎯

Responses

5 responses   15 responses   8 responses   12 responses

The average number of responses is 10

(i)   Name the reinforcement schedule used in A.

_____   (1)

(ii)   Name the reinforcement schedule used in B.

_____   (1)

(iii)   Explain why the two reinforcement schedules will produce different response patterns.

_____

_____   (3)

(e)   (i)   Using secondary reinforcement, such as tokens, how could you motivate people to pick up litter?

_____

_____

_____   (4)

(ii)   "A token economy leads to token learning."

The person who said this was making a criticism of the token economy system. Explain in your own words what was meant.

_____

_____   (3)

Chapter quiz

Answer the following questions in no longer than 10 minutes:

1   What name is given to the relationship between the strength of a response and the similarity of the stimulus to the original one?
2   What type of physiological response did Menzies condition?
3   What unconditioned stimulus did Volkova use?
4   Which type of conditioning is it if the conditioned stimulus is over before the unconditioned stimulus occurs?
5   What law of learning did Thorndike discover?
6   What type of reinforcement schedule involves reinforcement being given after a set period of time?
7   What name is given to reinforcement which satisfies a basic need?
8   What name is given to the type of learning which involves a sudden realisation of the solution?
9   What type of animal did Harlow use to demonstrate learning sets?
10   What form of mental representation did Tolman's studies of latent learning demonstrate?

Chapter 3 – Intelligence and other controversies

This chapter can be divided into three major segments, as follows:

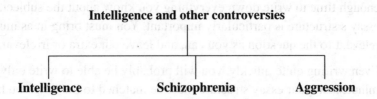

Intelligence and other controversies

Intelligence   **Schizophrenia**   **Aggression**

Each of those segments can then be subdivided into smaller tree diagrams. These can be useful in helping you to structure your revision.

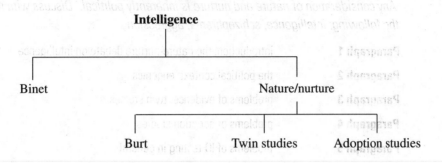

Intelligence

Binet

Nature/nurture

Burt   Twin studies   Adoption studies

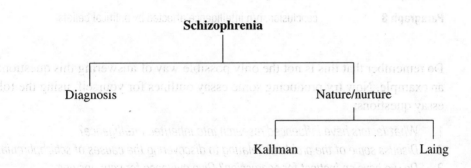

Schizophrenia

Diagnosis

Nature/nurture

Kallman   Laing

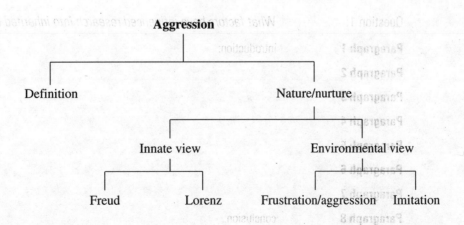

Aggression

Definition

Nature/nurture

Innate view   Environmental view

Freud   Lorenz   Frustration/aggression   Imitation

Planning an essay

When you are planning an essay for an examination, remember that you won't have enough time to write down everything you know about the subject. This means that the essay's structure is particularly important. You must bring in as much information that is relevant to the question as you can, and leave out extra or irrelevant details.

Even writing quite quickly, you will probably be able to write only one paragraph in five minutes, so your essay structure must be matched to the time you have available and you should plan what the paragraphs will cover with that in mind. Using this method, a 45-minute essay involves five minutes' thinking time and produces eight paragraphs. For example:

'Any consideration of nature and nurture is inherently political.' Discuss with reference to one of the following: intelligence, schizophrenia, aggression.

Paragraph 1	introduction: the nature-nurture debate on intelligence
Paragraph 2	the political context: eugenics
Paragraph 3	problems of evidence: twin studies
Paragraph 4	problems of adoption studies
Paragraph 5	problems of IQ testing in general
Paragraph 6	applications: e.g., streamed/segregated schooling
Paragraph 7	Binet's original criteria for testing
Paragraph 8	conclusion: n/n intelligence affected by political beliefs

Do remember that this is not the only possible way of answering this question: it is only an example. Now try producing some essay outlines for yourself, using the following essay questions:

1   What factors have influenced research into inherited intelligence?
2   Discuss some of the problems relating to discovering the causes of schizophrenia.
3   Do we have an instinct for aggression? Give evidence for your answer.
4   Discuss the idea that the entire nature-nurture distinction is a biological myth.

Question 1:	What factors have influenced research into inherited intelligence?
Paragraph 1	introduction:
Paragraph 2	
Paragraph 3	
Paragraph 4	
Paragraph 5	
Paragraph 6	
Paragraph 7	
Paragraph 8	conclusion:
Question 2:	Discuss some of the problems relating to discovering the causes of schizophrenia.
Paragraph 1	introduction:
Paragraph 2	
Paragraph 3	

Paragraph 4

Paragraph 5

Paragraph 6

Paragraph 7

Paragraph 8   conclusion:

Question 3:   *Do we have an instinct for aggression? Give evidence for your answer.*

Paragraph 1   introduction:

Paragraph 2

Paragraph 3

Paragraph 4

Paragraph 5

Paragraph 6

Paragraph 7

Paragraph 8   conclusion:

Question 4:   *Discuss the idea that the entire nature-nurture distinction is a biological myth.*

Paragraph 1   introduction:

Paragraph 2

Paragraph 3

Paragraph 4

Paragraph 5

Paragraph 6

Paragraph 7

Paragraph 8   conclusion:

Chapter summary

(*Psychology: an Introduction*, page 44)

1   Intelligence testing was first developed in order to identify children who needed special help with schooling.

2   Ideas of inherited intelligence developed through the work of Galton and his followers. The most influential of these was Cyril Burt, but he committed fraud in obtaining his data.

3   Obtaining evidence for the nature-nurture debate on intelligence is extremely difficult. Most of the studies are inadequate as evidence.

4   Ideas that schizophrenia is inherited have been very popular but the evidence rests on very wide definitions of 'schizophrenic'.

5   Laing suggested that schizophrenia could arise from family interactions. Rose et al. suggest that the interaction between physiology and experience is most important.

6   Freud and Lorenz saw aggression as an instinctive drive in human beings and suggested that channelling aggression safely was necessary for society.

7   Other studies have emphasised the way that aggression seems to arise as a response to frustrating circumstances, rather than automatically.

Key sections for revision

1 intelligence tests
2 Galton and Burt
3 nature/nurture intelligence
4 twin studies of schizophrenia
5 family interaction and schizophrenia
6 aggression as instinctive
7 frustration and aggression

Issues and perspectives

Using the following table, note down any features of interest which relate to the key sections of the chapter.

Key section	Methods of study	Evaluation and criticism	Ethical issues
1 intelligence tests			
2 Galton and Burt			
3 nature/nurture intelligence			
4 twin studies of schizophrenia			
5 family interaction and schizophrenia			
6 aggression as instinctive			
7 frustration and aggression			

Revision questions

Short-answer questions are useful for testing your knowledge of an area while you are revising, and for making sure that you understand it. They also often appear in examinations, and when they do you will have only a limited amount of time to answer them. The questions will be marked according to the information you have used to answer them and what you can attain marks for will be set out in a mark scheme.

Here are two 10-mark questions, with typical marking schemes which an examiner might use to assess answers.

Describe and discuss Rosenhan's study of schizophrenia diagnosis.

description of study	(up to)	4 marks
outcome of study	(up to)	3 marks
implications of study	(up to)	3 marks
		Total 10 marks

Compare and contrast biological and learning explanations for aggression.

biological explanation	(up to)	3 marks
learning explanation	(up to)	3 marks
similarities/differences	(up to)	4 marks
		Total 10 marks

As you can see, each question has its own mark scheme and these share out the marks between the different types of knowledge needed to answer the question.

Bearing this in mind, try to work out your own mark schemes for each of the following questions. Each question is worth 10 marks. If you feel that you need more help, look at the mark schemes in the other chapters.

1   *Discuss the advantages and disadvantages of twin studies of intelligence.*

2   *Distinguish between Binet's and Burt's views of intelligence.*

3   *Describe <u>either</u> the biological approach to schizophrenia <u>or</u> Laing's view of schizophrenia.*

4   *Describe Calhoun's study of aggression in rats.*

5   *Briefly discuss the social implications of the nature-nurture debates on intelligence, schizophrenia and aggression.*

When you have written your mark scheme, turn to the relevant pages in your textbook and make sure that your scheme reflects the information covered by that topic.

Answering revision questions

Now try answering each of these questions, giving yourself 15 minutes to complete each one. At the end of that time, mark your answer, using the mark scheme that you have developed.

(NB: It is essential that you write the mark scheme before you try to answer the question! Doing it the other way round would be completely pointless because you would be too influenced by what you have already written.)

1   Discuss the advantages and disadvantages of twin studies of intelligence.

2   Distinguish between Binet's and Burt's views of intelligence.

3   Describe <u>either</u> the biological approach to schizophrenia <u>or</u> Laing's view of schizophrenia.

4   Describe Calhoun's study of aggression in rats.

5   Briefly discuss the social implications of the nature-nurture debates on intelligence, schizophrenia and aggression.

A suggestion for practical work

This study has been derived from Exercise 3.1 suggested on page 35 of *Psychology: an Introduction*. It is an experiment which will allow you to see whether practice makes a difference in taking intelligence tests.

Carrying out the study

In planning your study, you will need to identify the following (consult Chapter 22, pages 424–8 of *Psychology: an Introduction* if you need further explanation):

hypothesis _____

null hypothesis _____

independent variable _____

dependent variable _____

design _____

controls _____

ethical considerations _____

_____

_____

_____

_____

_____

Make notes on how you will carry out this research. _____

_____

_____

_____

_____

Analysing the results

You will need a summary table of results which includes the mean, median and mode for your two sets of scores. It should be called Table 1 and will need a title telling your reader exactly what it is about. Use the instructions in Appendix 2A (page 205) to draw up your table.

You will also need a diagram to display your findings visually. For this, you will need to use a bar chart. One of the bars will represent the scores on the first occasion, and the other will represent the scores on the second occasion. This will be called Fig. 1. Use the instructions in Appendix 2B (page 205) to draw up a bar chart for your results.

Reporting the study

You are now ready to write up your study using the correct format. Use Checklist A, in Appendix 3 (page 210), to make sure you have included everything you need.

Sample examination questions

Midlands Examining Group, February 1990
Individual Differences Module, Source C, Questions 10–13
Paper reference: 723

Intelligence

Individuals differ in their intellectual ability. Psychologists have tried to explain how these differences occur. Are they genetic or are they due to environmental factors? One way to study the nature/nurture debate in intelligence is to look at adoption studies. In one study done in America, 130 black children were adopted by white middle class families who already had a child of their own. The researcher then gave the parents and the children an IQ test and correlated their scores. They found that the child was similar to the mother in IQ regardless of whether the child was adopted or biological. The results are show below in the table.

Relationship	Correlation result
Mother and biological child	.34 (weak positive correlation)
Mother and adopted child	.29 (weak positive correlation)
Father and biological child	.34 (weak positive correlation)
Father and adopted child	.07 (no correlation)

10   The families used in this study were all white and middle class. Why could this be a problem?

_____

_____   [2]

11   (a)   According to the table, what is the correlation between the IQ of the father and the adopted child?

_____   [1]

    (b)   How could you explain this correlation?

_____   [1]

12   What is meant by the term positive correlation?

_____

_____

_____   [3]

13   Describe, using examples, some of the other ways in which psychologists have tried to study the influence of heredity and environment on intelligence.

_____

_____

_____

_____

_____

_____

_____

_____

_____   [9]

Chapter quiz

Answer the following questions in no longer than 10 minutes:

1   Binet used the concept of _____ to assess intelligence.

2   What is the name of the hereditarian political movement supported by Galton?

3   Which psychologist came under suspicion of having falsified the results of twin studies?

4   What term is used to describe twins who have come from the same egg and are genetically identical?

5   Which illness did Kallman insist was inherited?

6   Who suggested that a 'retreat into madness' was often the only way of coping with intolerable social stress?

7   What name did Lorenz give to inherited actions which were supposed to stop an attack by another member of the same species?

8   What is the name for the idea that aggression may arise from difficult or stressful circumstances?

9   Who studied overcrowding in rats?

10 What technical name is given to theories which emphasise the importance of personal experience and learning?

This chapter can be divided into two major segments, as follows:

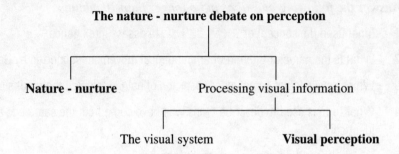

Each of those segments can then be subdivided into smaller tree diagrams. These can be useful in helping you to structure your revision.

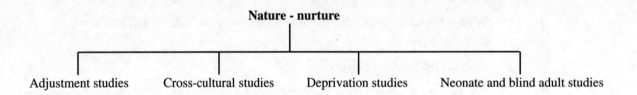

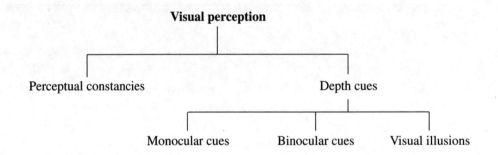

Planning an essay

When you are planning an essay for an examination, remember that you won't have enough time to write down everything you know about the subject. This means that the essay's structure is particularly important. You must bring in as much information that is relevant to the question as you can, and leave out extra or irrelevant details.

Even writing quite quickly, you will probably be able to write only one paragraph in five minutes so your essay structure must be matched to the time you have available and you should plan what the paragraphs will cover with that in mind. Using this method, a 45-minute essay involves five minutes' thinking time and produces eight paragraphs. For example:

SAMPLE QUESTION

To what extent can it be said that perceptual abilities are learned?

Paragraph 1	introduction: nature-nurture perception
Paragraph 2	adjusting perception: studies with goggles
Paragraph 3	environmental factors: cross-cultural studies
Paragraph 4	development: neonates and patterns
Paragraph 5	size and shape constancy (Bower)
Paragraph 6	need for activity: animal studies
Paragraph 7	blind people with restored vision
Paragraph 8	conclusion: partly innate, partly learned

Do remember that this is not the only possible way of answering this question: it is only an example. Now try producing some essay outlines for yourself, using the following questions:

1   *What evidence is there for innate perception in human infants?*
2   *How do we perceive depth?*
3   *What can visual illusions tell us about human perception?*
4   *How do we come to perceive sounds?*

Question 1:   *What evidence is there for innate perception in human infants?*

Paragraph 1	introduction:
Paragraph 2	
Paragraph 3	
Paragraph 4	
Paragraph 5	
Paragraph 6	
Paragraph 7	
Paragraph 8	conclusion:

Question 2:   *How do we perceive depth?*

Paragraph 1	introduction:
Paragraph 2	
Paragraph 3	

Paragraph 4

Paragraph 5

Paragraph 6

Paragraph 7

Paragraph 8   conclusion:

Question 3:   *What can visual illusions tell us about human perception?*

Paragraph 1   introduction:

Paragraph 2

Paragraph 3

Paragraph 4

Paragraph 5

Paragraph 6

Paragraph 7

Paragraph 8   conclusion:

Question 4:   *How do we come to perceive sounds?*

Paragraph 1   introduction:

Paragraph 2

Paragraph 3

Paragraph 4

Paragraph 5

Paragraph 6

Paragraph 7

Paragraph 8   conclusion:

Chapter summary

(*Psychology: an Introduction*, page 62)

1   Distortion and readjustment studies suggest that human perception is flexible, which suggests that it is probably not inherited.

2   Deprivation and cross-cultural studies emphasise the need for certain forms of experience in developing accurate perception.

3   Studies of neonates have shown that some basic perceptual processes, such as size constancy or depth perception, may be inherited.

4   An investigation of a blind man given sight when mature indicated the importance of motivation in the development of perception.

5   The visual system organises light information in the eye and passes it on to the lateral geniculate bodies of the thalamus and then to the visual cortex of the brain for interpretation.

6   We can learn a great deal about how perception works through studying visual illusions, and identifying why it has gone wrong.

7   We can judge the direction of sounds because we have two separate ears, and distance through the fading out of the signal.

Key sections for revision

1   distortion and readjustment studies
2   deprivation and cross-cultural studies
3   neonate studies
4   studies of blind people
5   the visual system
6   visual illusions
7   auditory perception

Issues and perspectives

Using the following table, note down any features of interest which relate to the key sections of the chapter.

Key section	Methods of study	Evaluation and criticism	Ethical issues
1 distortion and readjustment studies			
2 deprivation and cross-cultural studies			
3 neonate studies			
4 studies of blind people			
5 the visual system			
6 visual illusions			
7 auditory perception			

Revision questions

Short-answer questions are useful for testing your knowledge of an area while you are revising, and for making sure that you understand it. They also often appear in examinations, and when they do you will have only a limited amount of time to answer them. The questions will be marked according to the information you have used to answer them and what you can attain marks for will be set out in a mark scheme.

Here are two 10-mark questions, with typical marking schemes which an examiner might use to assess answers.

Outline the main methods of studying the nature-nurture debate on perception.

deprivation studies	(up to)	2 marks
neonate studies	(up to)	2 marks
cross-cultural studies	(up to)	2 marks
distortion/readjustment studies	(up to)	2 marks
restored vision studies	(up to)	2 marks
		Total 10 marks

How do we detect the location of a sound?

transduction		1 mark
physical structure of ear	(up to)	2 marks
neural pathways/cortex	(up to)	3 marks
distance (attenuation)	(up to)	2 marks
orientation (discrepancy)	(up to)	2 marks
		Total 10 marks

As you can see, each question has its own mark scheme and these share out the marks between the different types of knowledge needed to answer the question.

Bearing this in mind, try to work out your own mark schemes for each of the following questions. Each question is worth 10 marks. If you feel that you need more help, look at the mark schemes in the other chapters.

1 *List the main perceptual depth cues and distinguish between monocular and binocular cues.*

2 *Describe a study of perception in adult humans.*

3 *Critically evaluate a study of perception in infancy.*

4 *What are perceptual constancies? Give specific examples.*

5 *Give two examples of visual illusions which arise from constancy scaling.*

When you have written your mark scheme, turn to the relevant pages in your textbook and make sure that your scheme reflects the information covered by that topic.

Answering revison questions

Now try answering each of these questions, giving yourself 15 minutes to complete each one. At the end of that time, mark your answer, using the mark scheme that you have developed.

(NB: It is essential that you write the mark scheme before you try to answer the question! Doing it the other way round would be completely pointless because you would be too influenced by what you have already written.)

QUESTIONS

1   List the main perceptual depth cues and distinguish between monocular and binocular cues.

2   Describe a study of perception in adult humans.

3   Critically evaluate a study of perception in infancy.

4   What are perceptual constancies? Give specific examples.

5   Give <u>two</u> examples of visual illusions which arise from constancy scaling.

A suggestion for practical work

This study has been derived from Exercise 4.1 suggested on page 49 of *Psychology: an Introduction*. It is an experiment which allows you to investigate people's responses to the Müller-Lyer illusion.

If Gregory's explanation is correct, a vertical illusion should be stronger than a horizontal one because it is more like its real-life equivalent. So, in this study you can compare people's responses to the Müller-Lyer illusion when it is presented vertically and when it is presented horizontally.

Carrying out the study

In planning your study, you will need to identify the following (consult Chapter 22, pages 424–8 of *Psychology: an Introduction* if you need further explanation):

hypothesis _____

null hypothesis _____

independent variable _____

dependent variable _____

design _____

controls _____

ethical considerations _____

_____

_____

_____

Make notes on how you will carry out this research. _____

_____

_____

_____

_____

Analysing the results

You will need a summary table of results which includes the mean, median and mode for your two groups. It needs to be called Table 1 and will need a title telling your reader exactly what it is about. Use the instructions in Appendix 2A (page 205) to draw up your table.

You will also need a diagram to display your findings visually. For this, you will need to use a bar chart. One of the bars will represent the vertical scores and the other will represent the horizontal ones. This will be called Fig. 1. Use the instructions in Appendix 2B (page 205) to draw up a bar chart for your results.

Reporting the study

You are now ready to write up your study using the correct format. Use Checklist A, in Appendix 3 (page 210), to make sure you have included everything you need.

Sample examination question

Northern Examining Association, June 1991
Paper 2, Question 5
Paper reference: 2175

5

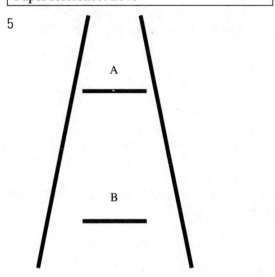

(a) Name one monocular depth cue to be found in the above illusion.

_____ [1]

(b) How have psychologists used the theory of size constancy to explain the illusion that line A seems to be longer than line B?

_____

_____

_____

[4]

"I SCREAM" and "ICE CREAM" produce the same sensation but when spoken in the sentences above are perceived differently.

(c) What is the term for the above effect?

_____ [1]

(d) Use the above example to explain the difference between sensation and perception.

_____

_____

_____ [3]

(e) Describe a study which suggests that previous experience affects perception.

_____

_____

_____

_____

_____ [5]

(f) When a person closes one eye some but not all of the ability to perceive depth is lost. Use psychological theory to explain this.

_____

_____

_____

_____

_____ [6]

Chapter quiz

Answer the following questions in no longer than 10 minutes:

1 Who studied perception by using red-green goggles?

2 What name was given to the apparatus used by Held and Hein?

3 Which Canadian people were not fooled by the Müller-Lyer illusion?

4 Who designed the visual cliff?

5 What kind of perception did Fantz demonstrate in infants?

6 What name is given to our ability to perceive colour accurately even if the wavelengths our eyes receive imply a different colour?

7 Which type of depth cue involves the use of both eyes?

8 Which species is better at distinguishing the direction of sounds: dogs or humans?

9 Which area of the cerebrum processes visual information?

10 What game did Bower use to test infant size constancy?

Chapter 5 – How the brain works

This chapter can be divided into two major segments, as follows:

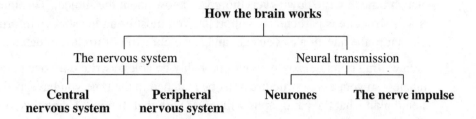

Each of those segments can then be subdivided into smaller tree diagrams. These can be useful in helping you to structure your revision.

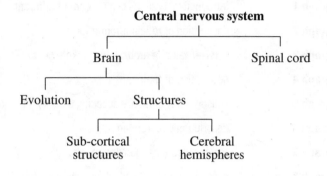

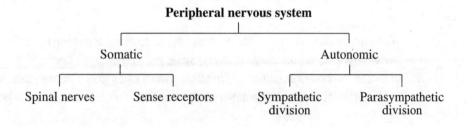

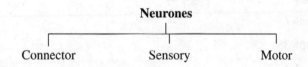

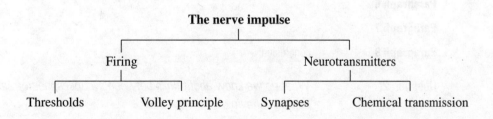

Planning an essay

When you are planning an essay for an examination, remember that you won't have enough time to write down everything you know about the subject. This means that the essay's structure is particularly important. You must bring in as much information that is relevant to the question as you can, and leave out extra or irrelevant details.

Even writing quite quickly, you will probably be able to write only one paragraph in five minutes, so your essay structure must be matched to the time you have available and you should plan what the paragraphs will cover with that in mind. Using this method, a 45-minute essay involves five minutes' thinking time and produces eight paragraphs. For example:

Outline three structures of the brain and discuss their functioning.

Paragraph 1	introduction: brain as complex set of different structures working together
Paragraph 2	description of reticular formation
Paragraph 3	survival value of arousal and wakefulness
Paragraph 4	description of thalamus
Paragraph 5	sensory relay station – decoding sensory information
Paragraph 6	description of cerebrum
Paragraph 7	memory, learning, perception, etc.
Paragraph 8	conclusion: we are still a long way from knowing everything about the brain

Do remember that this is not the only possible way of answering this question: it is only an example. Now try producing some essay outlines for yourself, using the following questions:

QUESTIONS

1   *How can the different types of neurones help us to avoid or minimise pain?*
2   *What do we know about links between synapses, neurotransmitters and human behaviour?*
3   *How can the brain's structure and function give us clues to evolutionary development?*
4   *What different parts of the brain might be involved in an activity such as washing up?*

Question 1:	*How can the different types of neurones help us to avoid or minimise pain?*
Paragraph 1	introduction:
Paragraph 2	
Paragraph 3	
Paragraph 4	
Paragraph 5	
Paragraph 6	
Paragraph 7	
Paragraph 8	conclusion:
Question 2:	*What do we know about links between synapses, neurotransmitters and human behaviour?*
Paragraph 1	introduction:
Paragraph 2	
Paragraph 3	
Paragraph 4	

Paragraph 5

Paragraph 6

Paragraph 7

Paragraph 8　　　　conclusion:

Question 3:　　　　*How can the brain's structure and function give us clues to evolutionary development?*

Paragraph 1　　　　introduction:

Paragraph 2

Paragraph 3

Paragraph 4

Paragraph 5

Paragraph 6

Paragraph 7

Paragraph 8　　　　conclusion:

Question 4:　　　　*What different parts of the brain might be involved in an activity such as washing up?*

Paragraph 1　　　　introduction:

Paragraph 2

Paragraph 3

Paragraph 4

Paragraph 5

Paragraph 6

Paragraph 7

Paragraph 8　　　　conclusion:

Chapter summary

(*Psychology: an Introduction*, page 87)

1　The nervous system can be divided into the central and peripheral nervous systems. The central nervous system consists of the brain and the spinal cord; the peripheral nervous system consists of the somatic and autonomic nervous systems.

2　There are three main types of neurones: connector neurones, sensory neurones and motor neurones. Together, these form the reflex arc.

3　Neurones connect by means of synapses. Neurotransmitters are chemicals which pass messages from one neurone to another. Different neurotransmitters have different effects.

4　The brain works by means of electrical messages which are passed from one neurone to another. Information is coded so that the brain can interpret the information which it receives from the sensory cells.

5　There are different structures in the brain itself, which mediate different functions. The oldest part of the brain consists of the medulla, cerebellum, pons and the reticular formation.

6　The middle part of the brain consists of the thalamus, limbic system and hypothalamus. It mediates slightly more sophisticated functions than the older part.

7　The most recent part of the brain is the cerebrum which mediates cognitive processes.

Key sections for revision

1   the nervous system
2   types of neurones
3   synapses and neurotransmitters
4   the nerve impulse
5   sub-cortical structures 1
6   sub-cortical structures 2
7   the cerebral hemispheres

Issues and perspectives

Using the following table, note down any features of interest which relate to the key sections of the chapter.

Key section	Methods of study	Evaluation and criticism	Ethical issues
1 the nervous system			
2 types of neurones			
3 synapses and neurotransmitters			
4 the nerve impulse			
5 sub-cortical structures 1			
6 sub-cortical structures 2			
7 the cerebral hemispheres			

Revision questions

Short-answer questions are useful for testing your knowledge of an area while you are revising, and for making sure that you understand it. They also often appear in examinations, and when they do you will have only a limited amount of time to answer them. The questions will be marked according to the information you have used to answer them, and what you can attain marks for will be set out in a mark scheme.

Here are two 10-mark questions, with typical marking schemes which an examiner might use to assess answers.

Outline the structure of the nervous system.

definition and function of nervous system	(up to)	2 marks
central nervous system	(up to)	2 marks
somatic nervous system	(up to)	2 marks
autonomic nervous system	(up to)	4 marks
		Total 10 marks

What are the functions of the cerebellum and reticular formation?

description/location of each	(up to)	2 marks
cerebellum: function	(up to)	3 marks
reticular formation: function	(up to)	3 marks
interaction with other areas	(up to)	2 marks
		Total 10 marks

As you can see, each question has its own mark scheme and these share out the marks among the different types of knowledge needed to answer the question.

Bearing this in mind, try to work out your own mark schemes for each of the following questions. Each question is worth 10 marks. If you feel that you need more help, look at the mark schemes in the other chapters.

1   *Draw a labelled diagram of a synapse, indicating the direction of the nerve impulse.*

2   *Describe the nervous system's involvement in pulling your hand away from a hot iron.*

3   *How are sounds converted into brain activity?*

4   *Discuss the location and functions of the thalamus.*

5   *Describe the structure and functions of the cerebral hemispheres.*

When you have written your mark scheme, turn to the relevant pages in your textbook and make sure that your scheme reflects the information covered by that topic.

Answering revision questions

Now try answering each of these questions, giving yourself 15 minutes to complete each one. At the end of that time, mark your answer, using the mark scheme that you have developed.

(NB: It is essential that you write the mark scheme before you try to answer the question! Doing it the other way round would be completely pointless because you would be too influenced by what you have already written.)

1   *Draw a labelled diagram of a synapse, indicating the direction of the nerve impulse.*

2   *Describe the nervous system's involvement in pulling your hand away from a hot iron.*

3   *How are sounds converted into brain activity?*

4   *Discuss the location and functions of the thalamus.*

5   *Describe the structure and functions of the cerebral hemispheres.*

A suggestion for practical work

This study has been derived from Exercise 5.2 suggested on page 78 of *Psychology: an Introduction*. It is an experiment which will allow you to investigate practice and reaction time.

In the first condition, you will need to obtain a set of scores from people who have not practised the task. Then give them an opportunity to practise (say, 10 times) before obtaining a set of scores after practising. Have they improved?

Carrying out the study

In planning your study, you will need to identify the following (consult Chapter 22, pages 424–8 of *Psychology: an Introduction* if you need further explanation):

hypothesis _____

null hypothesis _____

independent variable _____

dependent variable _____

controls _____

ethical considerations _____

_____

_____

_____

Make notes on how you will carry out this research. _____

_____

_____

_____

Analysing the results

You will need a summary table of results which includes the mean, median and mode for your two groups. It should be called Table 1 and will need a title telling your reader exactly what it is about. Use the instructions in Appendix 2A (page 205) to draw up your table.

You will also need a diagram to display your findings visually. For this, you will need to use a graph which presents the average score for each of the practice occasions as well as for the test ones. The bottom line will, therefore, represent the number of times people have practised the task. This graph will be called Fig.1. Use the instructions in Appendix 2C (page 207) to draw up a graph for your results.

Reporting the study

You are now ready to write up your study using the correct format. Use Checklist A, in Appendix 3 (page 210), to make sure you have included everything you need.

Sample examination questions

Midlands Examining Group, June 1988
Physiological Module, Source D, Questions 14/18
Paper reference: 620

When Sarah was two years old, she suffered from a rare type of brain infection that gave her a high fever. It seemed that she had recovered entirely until, at the age of ten, she began to have attacks of either extreme rage or fear. The doctors concluded that the illness had left her with a damaged brain.

When Sarah was 16, she began to carry a pocket-knife. One evening at the cinema, Sarah began to feel sick and went to the toilet. A girl bumped into her and Sarah pulled out her knife and stabbed the girl several times.

An EEG was done to record the electrical charges in Sarah's temporal lobe. The doctors decided to stimulate electrically the amygdala which is part of the limbic system. Research with animals showed that stimulation of the amygdala caused rage while removal of the amygdala makes animals very tame. When the doctors stimulated Sarah's amygdala, she flew into a violent rage. The doctors decided that her attacks were caused by scar tissue which had formed in the amygdala. They used an electrical current to destroy the scar tissue and Sarah showed no further attacks.

14   What behaviour did Sarah show at the age of 10?

_____ [1]

15   According to the animal studies, what effect does removing the amygdala have on the animals' behaviour?

_____ [1]

16   What effect did electrically stimulating the amygdala have on Sarah's behaviour

_____ [1]

17   Describe two other methods of investigating the brain.

_____

_____

_____

_____ [4]

18   Choose any two of the following brain structures and explain how each one affects human behaviour:

thalamus

_____

_____

cerebellum

_____

_____

hypothalamus

_____

_____

cerebrum

_____

_____   [8]

Chapter quiz

Answer the following questions in no longer than 10 minutes:

1   The central nervous system consists of the brain and which other structure?

2   Which is the third type of neurone: motor, sensory and   ?

3   What does a synaptic vesicle hold?

4   What name is given to the period immediately after a nerve cell has fired, during which it cannot fire again?

5   What name is given to the fatty covering on the axon of many neurones?

6   Which neurotransmitter is found at the motor end-plate?

7   Which structure joins the two halves of the cerebrum?

8   What is the general term for the areas of the brain which lie below the cerebrum?

9   What two types of information do sound waves carry?

10   What do we call the conversion of a stimulus into electrical impulses?

Chapter 6 – Emotion and arousal

This chapter can be divided into two major segments, as follows:

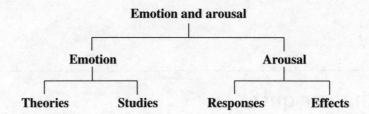

Each of those segments can then be subdivided into smaller tree diagrams. These can be useful in helping you to structure your revision.

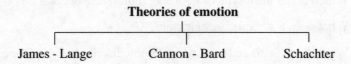

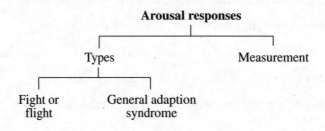

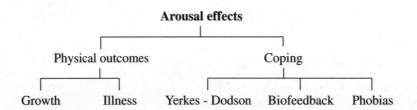

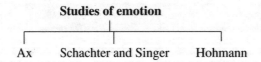

Planning an essay

When you are planning an essay for an examination, remember that you won't have enough time to write down everything you know about the subject. This means that the essay's structure is particularly important. You must bring in as much information that is relevant to the question as you can, and leave out extra or irrelevant details.

Even writing quite quickly, you will probably be able to write only one paragraph in five minutes, so your essay structure must be matched to the time you have available, and you should plan what the paragraphs will cover with that in mind. Using this method, a 45-minute essay involves five minutes' thinking time and produces eight paragraphs. For example:

Describe the changes that occur during the 'fight or flight' response. How far would you consider these changes to be an important part of emotion?

Paragraph 1	introduction: fight or flight as a survival mechanism
Paragraph 2	the autonomic nervous system: sympathetic and parasympathetic divisions
Paragraph 3	symptoms of 'fight or flight'
Paragraph 4	James-Lange theory
Paragraph 5	Cannon-Bard theory
Paragraph 6	Schachter and Singer's study
Paragraph 7	another study (e.g., Hohmann, Valins, etc.)
Paragraph 8	Conclusion: emotion as a mixture of cognitive and physiological reactions

Of course, this isn't the only way of answering this question: it's only an example. Now try producing some essay outlines for yourself, using the following questions:

1   *How can we measure emotional arousal and why would we want to do so?*
2   *Discuss some of the consequences of long-term stress. How can a knowledge of psychology help people experiencing long-term stress?*
3   *Outline some treatments for phobias and discuss the psychological principles on which they are based.*
4   *What explanations have been put forward for why we experience fear or anger?*

Question 1:	*How can we measure emotional arousal and why would we want to do so?*
Paragraph 1	introduction:
Paragraph 2	
Paragraph 3	
Paragraph 4	
Paragraph 5	
Paragraph 6	
Paragraph 7	
Paragraph 8	conclusion:

Question 2:	*Discuss some of the consequences of long-term stress. How can a knowledge of psychology help people experiencing long-term stress?*
Paragraph 1	introduction:
Paragraph 2	
Paragraph 3	

Paragraph 4

Paragraph 5

Paragraph 6

Paragraph 7

Paragraph 8   conclusion:

Question 3:   *Outline some treatments for phobias and discuss the psychological principles on which they are based.*

Paragraph 1   introduction:

Paragraph 2

Paragraph 3

Paragraph 4

Paragraph 5

Paragraph 6

Paragraph 7

Paragraph 8   conclusion:

Question 4:   *What explanations have been put forward for why we experience fear or anger?*

Paragraph 1   introduction:

Paragraph 2

Paragraph 3

Paragraph 4

Paragraph 5

Paragraph 6

Paragraph 7

Paragraph 8   conclusion:

Chapter summary

(*Psychology: an Introduction*, page 105)

1   Emotions like fear or anger produce an alarm reaction in the body, which is the activation of the sympathetic division of the autonomic nervous system.

2   Arousal may be measured by galvanic skin response (GSR) or other techniques. Polygraphs or lie-detectors measure arousal.

3   Long-term stress has been shown to lead to illnesses such as heart attacks or stomach ulcers. Biofeedback is one way of dealing with the control of stress.

4   Phobias (extreme irrational fears) may be treated by therapies designed to reduce the levels of arousal by conditioning.

5   Various theories have been put forward to explain how we feel emotion. The James-Lange theory stated that we feel the physiological change first and then interpret it as the emotion.

6   The Cannon-Bard theory stated that physiological reactions and our feelings of emotion happen totally separately.

7   Schachter and Singer's theory stated that the social situation affects the type of emotion that we feel but the physiological changes affect how intensely we feel it.

Key sections for revision

1   the autonomic nervous system
2   measuring arousal
3   stress
4   treatments for phobias
5   the James-Lange theory of emotion
6   the Cannon-Bard theory of emotion
7   Schachter and Singer's theory of emotion

Issues and perspectives

Using the following table, note down any features of interest which relate to the key sections of the chapter.

Key section	Methods of study	Evaluation and criticism	Ethical issues
1 the autonomic nervous system			
2 measuring arousal			
3 stress			
4 treatments for phobias			
5 the James-Lange theory			
6 the Cannon-Bard theory			
7 Schachter and Singer's theory			

Revision questions

Short-answer questions are useful for testing your knowledge of an area while you are revising, and for making sure that you understand it. They also often appear in examinations, and when they do you will have only a limited amount of time to answer them. The questions will be marked according to the information you have used to answer them and what you can attain marks for will be set out in a mark scheme.

Here are two 10-mark questions, with typical marking schemes which an examiner might use to assess answers.

Outline and discuss three different treatments for phobias.

description of desensitisation	(up to)	3 marks
description of implosion therapy	(up to)	2 marks
description of modelling/other equivalent	(up to)	2 marks
comparison/discussion	(up to)	3 marks
		Total 10 marks

Describe and evaluate Schachter and Singer's study of emotion.

description of study	(up to)	4 marks
outcomes of study	(up to)	3 marks
implications/discussion	(up to)	3 marks
		Total 10 marks

As you can see, each question has its own mark scheme and these share out the marks between the different types of knowledge needed to answer the question.

Bearing this in mind, try to work out your own mark schemes for each of the following questions. Each question is worth 10 marks. If you feel that you need more help, look at the mark schemes in the other chapters.

1 *Describe the main feature of the alarm reaction.*

2 *How can physiological arousal be measured?*

3 *How did Friedman and Rosenman help us to understand long-term stress?*

4 *Distinguish between the James-Lange and Cannon-Bard theories of emotion.*

5 *Describe Ax's study of emotional responses.*

When you have written your mark scheme, turn to the relevant pages in your textbook and make sure that your scheme reflects the information covered by that topic.

Answering revision questions

Now try answering each of these questions, giving yourself 15 minutes to complete each one. At the end of that time, mark your answer, using the mark scheme that you have developed.

(NB: It is essential that you write the mark scheme before you try to answer the question! Doing it the other way round would be completely pointless because you would be too influenced by what you have already written.)

1   *Describe the main feature of the alarm reaction.*

2   *How can physiological arousal be measured?*

3   *How did Friedman and Rosenman help us to understand long-term stress?*

4   *Distinguish between the James-Lange and Cannon-Bard theories of emotion.*

5   *Describe Ax's study of emotional responses.*

A suggestion for practical work

This study has been derived from Exercise 6.1 suggested on page 91 of *Psychology: an Introduction*. It is an experiment which will allow you to look at how arousal levels change when we are faced with frustrating events.

You will need to carry out the study with several people, rather than just one or two, in order to be able to compare their results.

Carrying out the study

In planning your study, you will need to identify the following (consult Chapter 22, pages 424–8 of *Psychology: an Introduction* if you need further explanation):

hypothesis _____

null hypothesis _____

independent variable _____

dependent variable _____

design _____

controls _____

ethical considerations _____

_____

_____

_____

_____

Make notes on how you will carry out this study. _____

_____

_____

_____

_____

Analysing the results

You will need a summary table of results which includes the mean, median and mode for your two groups. It should be called Table 1 and will need a title telling your reader exactly what it is about. Look in Appendix 2A (page 205) for guidance in drawing up your table.

You will also need a diagram to display your findings visually. This will be called Fig. 1. Use a bar chart to show the mean scores from the two groups of people that you have studied. One of the bars will represent the mean score before the frustrating event and the other will represent the mean score afterwards. Appendix 2B (page 205) will help you to draw up your chart.

Reporting the study

You are now ready to write up your experiment in the correct format.

Use Checklist A in the Appendix (page 210) to make sure you have included everything you need to.

Sample examination question

Northern Examining Association, June 1991
Paper 2, Question 1
Paper reference: 2175

1 Subjects from three different countries, the United States, Italy and Japan, were each shown the following cartoon faces.

Face A   Face B

(a) Describe **two** differences between face A and face B.

_____

_____ [2]

(b) ALL of the subjects said that face A showed **anger** and face B showed **happiness**.

What do these results suggest about the facial expressions which show anger and happiness?

_____ [1]

(c) Facial expressions can be an unreliable guide to people's emotions. Explain why.

_____

_____ [2]

(d) Two groups of people had spinal cord damage.

Group A had spinal cord damage near the neck.

Group B had spinal cord damage near the bottom of the spine.

The people in each group were asked to rate how angry they get nowadays compared with how angry they used to get before their injury.

The results are shown in the graph below.

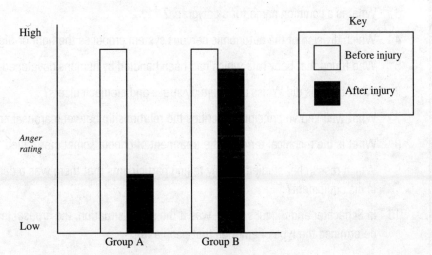

(i) Describe the results in words.

_____

_____ [2]

(ii) Explain why the difference between the two groups occurred.

_____

_____ [3]

(e) Describe any **one** study which shows that a situation can affect the type of emotion a person feels.

_____

_____

_____ [4]

(f) The diagram below illustrates a theory of emotion.

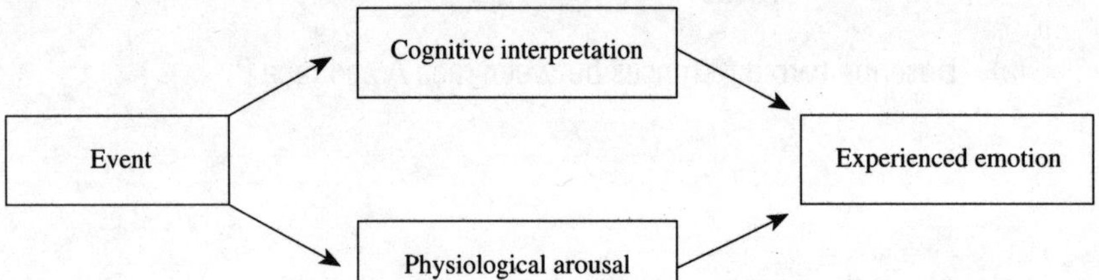

Imagine that you are walking home alone one dark night. You hear a strange sound behind you. Name **one** emotion you might feel and use the theory shown in the diagram above to explain it.

_____

_____

_____ [6]

Chapter quiz

Answer the following questions in no longer than 10 minutes:

1 What reaction shows up in humans as 'goose-pimples'?

2 What does GAS stand for?

3 What is a common name for a polygraph?

4 Which division of the autonomic nervous system produces the fight or flight response?

5 Who found that baby rats which had been handled by humans developed faster?

6 What animals did Weiss use to study stress and stomach ulcers?

7 What well-known principle describes the relationship between arousal and performance?

8 What is the technical term for the treatment of phobia sometimes called 'flooding'?

9 Which researcher studied fear by telling participants that there was a dangerous short-circuit in his equipment?

10 In Schachter and Singer's study, was it the social situation, the arousal level or the drug which determined the type of emotion that people felt?

Chapter 7 – Sleep, dreaming and consciousness

This chapter can be divided into three major segments, as follows:

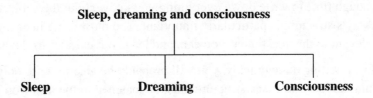

Each of those segments can then be subdivided into smaller tree diagrams. These can be useful in helping you to structure your revision.

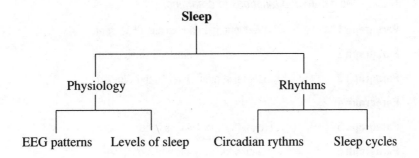

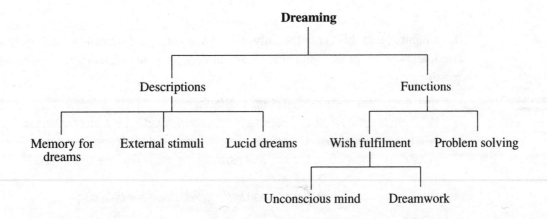

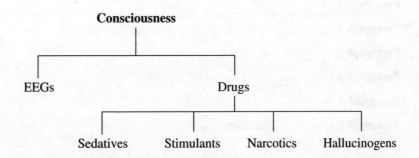

Planning an essay

When you are planning an essay for an examination, remember that you won't have enough time to write down everything you know about the subject. This means that the essay's structure is particularly important. You must bring in as much information that is relevant to the question as you can, and leave out extra or irrelevant details.

Even writing quite quickly, you will probably be able to write only one paragraph in five minutes, so your essay structure must be matched to the time you have available and you should plan what the paragraphs will cover with that in mind. Using this method, a 45-minute essay involves five minutes' thinking time and produces eight paragraphs. For example:

SAMPLE QUESTION

Discuss the nature and functions of dreaming.

Paragraph 1	introduction: dreaming and REM sleep
Paragraph 2	remembering dreams and sleep cycles
Paragraph 3	external stimuli: Dement and Wolpert
Paragraph 4	lucid dreams
Paragraph 5	Freud: the unconscious mind
Paragraph 6	dreamwork: symbols and archetypes
Paragraph 7	Evans: dreams as organising information
Paragraph 8	conclusion: dreaming as a distinctive state of consciousness

Do remember that this is not the only way of answering this question – it is only an example. Now try producing some essay outlines for yourself, using the following questions:

QUESTIONS

1 *How have researchers studied sleep and dreaming?*
2 *What are circadian rhythms? How may circadian rhythms affect human behaviour?*
3 *What have psychologists discovered about different states of consciousness?*
4 *What do we know about the way that psychoactive drugs produce their effects?*

Question 1:	*How have researchers studied sleep and dreaming?*
Paragraph 1	introduction:
Paragraph 2	
Paragraph 3	
Paragraph 4	
Paragraph 5	
Paragraph 6	
Paragraph 7	
Paragraph 8	conclusion:

Question 2:	*What are circadian rhythms? How may circadian rhythms affect human behaviour?*
Paragraph 1	introduction:
Paragraph 2	
Paragraph 3	
Paragraph 4	

Paragraph 5

Paragraph 6

Paragraph 7

Paragraph 8   conclusion:

Question 3:   *What have psychologists discovered about different states of consciousness?*

Paragraph 1   introduction:

Paragraph 2

Paragraph 3

Paragraph 4

Paragraph 5

Paragraph 6

Paragraph 7

Paragraph 8   conclusion:

Question 4:   *What do we know about the way that psychoactive drugs produce their effects?*

Paragraph 1   introduction:

Paragraph 2

Paragraph 3

Paragraph 4

Paragraph 5

Paragraph 6

Paragraph 7

Paragraph 8   conclusion:

Chapter summary

(*Psychology: an Introduction*, page 123)

1   Sleep takes place in cycles – while sleeping, we alternate between different levels of sleep. We also show diurnal or circadian rhythms in our pattern of sleep and wakefulness.

2   There are physiological correlates to sleep which mean that we can see, using EEG records, when people are deeply asleep and when they are dreaming.

3   Studies of dreaming have shown that external stimuli can be included in dreams and that people can learn to control lucid dreams.

4   Several different theories have been put forward to explain why we dream. Freud suggested that it was unconscious wish-fulfilment; but Evans suggested that it is our way of sorting out sensory information.

5   Early investigations of consciousness included the idea that consciousness comes from a combination of external sensations and internal states.

6   Investigations of consciousness have shown that different states of consciousness may connect with physiological indicators, like EEG patterns.

7   Psychoactive drugs such as stimulants, sedatives, narcotics and hallucinogens, can produce powerful changes in states of consciousness.

Key sections for revision

1   sleep cycles and diurnal rhythms
2   physiological correlates of sleep
3   studies of dreaming
4   theories of dreaming
5   states of consciousness
6   studying consciousness
7   psychoactive drugs

Issues and perspectives

Using the following table, note down any features of interest which relate to the key sections of the chapter.

Key section	Methods of study	Evaluation and criticism	Ethical issues
1 sleep cycles and diurnal rhythms			
2 physiological correlates of sleep			
3 studies of dreaming			
4 theories of dreaming			
5 states of consciousness			
6 studying consciousness			
7 psychoactive drugs			

Revision questions

Short-answer questions are useful for testing your knowledge of an area while you are revising, and for making sure that you understand it. They also often appear in examinations, and when they do you will have only a limited amount of time to answer them. The questions will be marked according to the information you have used to answer them and what you can attain marks for will be set out in a mark scheme.

Here are two 10-mark questions, with typical marking schemes which an examiner might use to assess answers.

Outline Freud's theory of dreaming.

Freud's model of mind	(up to)	3 marks
functions of dreaming	(up to)	3 marks
dreamwork	(up to)	4 marks
		Total 10 marks

What are the main groups of psychoactive drugs?

definition of psychoactive drugs	(up to)	2 marks
sedatives	(up to)	2 marks
stimulants	(up to)	2 marks
narcotics	(up to)	2 marks
hallucinogens	(up to)	2 marks
		Total 10 marks

As you can see, each question has its own mark scheme and these share out the marks between the different types of knowledge needed to answer the question.

Bearing this in mind, try to work out your own mark schemes for each of the following questions. Each question is worth 10 marks. If you feel that you need further help, look at the mark schemes in the other chapters.

1   *What are the major physiological correlates of sleep?*

2   *How are EEGs used to study consciousness and sleep?*

3   *Outline and discuss one example of disrupted circadian rhythms in normal life.*

4   *Describe and evaluate an experimental study of dreaming.*

5   *Compare and contrast the activity and effects of the drugs caffeine and alcohol.*

When you have written your mark scheme, turn to the relevant pages in your textbook and make sure that your scheme reflects the information covered by that topic.

Answering revision questions

Now try answering each of these questions, giving yourself 15 minutes to complete each one. At the end of that time, mark your answer, using the mark scheme that you have developed.

(NB: It is essential that you write the mark scheme <u>before</u> you try to answer the question! Doing it the other way round would be completely pointless because you would be too influenced by what you have already written.)

 **QUESTIONS**

1   *What are the major physiological correlates of sleep?*

2   *How are EEGs used to study consciousness and sleep?*

3   *Outline and discuss <u>one</u> example of disrupted circadian rhythms in normal life.*

4   *Describe and evaluate an experimental study of dreaming.*

5   *Compare and contrast the activity and effects of the drugs caffeine and alcohol.*

A suggestion for practical work

This study has been derived from Exercise 7.1 suggested on page 111 of *Psychology: an Introduction*. It is a case study which will allow you to correlate your own feelings of alertness with body temperature, to see if they indicate a systematic biological rhythm.

Carrying out the study

In planning your study, you will need to identify the following (consult Chapter 22, pages 424–8 of *Psychology: an Introduction* if you need further explanation):

hypothesis _____

null hypothesis _____

variable 1 _____

variable 2 _____

controls _____

ethical considerations _____

_____

_____

_____

_____

Make notes on how you will carry out this research. _____

_____

_____

_____

_____

Analysing the results

You will need a diagram to display your findings visually. This will be called Fig. 1. Use the notes in Appendix 2C (page 207) to help you to draw up a graph for these results. The graph will have two lines: one to represent your temperature and the other to represent alertness. The bottom line of the graph will represent the time when you took the measurements .

You should also draw up a scattergram to show the relationship between your two measurements. Use the notes in Appendix 2D (page 208) to help you to do this.

Reporting the study

You are now ready to write up your experiment in the correct format.

Use Checklist B in the Appendix (page 210) to make sure you have included everything you need to.

Sample examination questions

Midlands Examining Group, February 1989
Physiological Module, Source D, Questions 10/12
Paper reference: 680

The Classification of Drugs

10 All drugs can be classified by their effect on the central nervous system – whether they are stimulating or depressing. The chart shows a range of effects. Look at the list of drugs below.

(a) Write the name of each of these drugs in the appropriate box on the right-hand side of the chart. The example given is anaesthetics. These are placed at the depression end of the range because they have a depressing effect on the central nervous system, and produce a loss of feeling and sensation.   [6]

LIST OF DRUGS

Amphetamines
Minor tranquilisers (for example, valium)
Cocaine
Alcohol
Heroin and morphine

STIMULATION

PHYSICAL EFFECTS   DRUGS

Convulsions and Death

Extreme nervousness

Anxiety, palpitations

Feeling of well-being

Distortions of time and space

NEUTRAL AREA

Anxiety relief

Drowsiness

Sleep

Loss of pain

Loss of feelings and sensations

Convulsions and Death   Anaesthetics

DEPRESSION

(b) (i) Select any one of the five drugs listed above and answer Questions 11 and 12 with reference to that drug.

(ii) The drug I have selected is:

11 (a) What are the *psychological* effects of taking the drug you have selected?

_____

_____

_____   [2]

(b)   What are the *physical* effects of taking the drug you have selected?

_____

_____

_____

[2]

12   (a)   In what ways can the drug you have selected be used to help people?
     (b)   In what ways is this drug abused?
     (c)   What are the long term effects of abuse?

     (a)   *Helping people*

_____

_____

_____

_____

[3]

     (b)   *Abuse*

_____

_____

_____

_____

[3]

     (c)   *Long term effects of abuse*

_____

_____

_____

_____

[3]

Chapter quiz

Answer the following questions in no longer than 10 minutes:

1   If 'orthodox' is the term used for normal sleep, what term is used for REM sleep?

2   What general term is used to refer to the physical changes which are associated with sleep?

3   Which type of biological rhythm goes round the clock?

4   What is the common name for a disorder occurring as a result of disrupted biological rhythms?

5   What animals did French use to study the role of the RAS in sleep?

6   What do we call dreams in which we know that we are dreaming?

7   According to Freud, dreams involve hidden symbolic messages. What term describes the process of using symbols in this way?

8   Which group of drugs produces distortions of consciousness or enhanced perceptual awareness?

9   What type of EEG rhythm indicates that a person is awake but relaxed?

10   What type of drug is alcohol?

Chapter 8 – Cognitive functions and the brain

This chapter can be divided into two major segments, as follows:

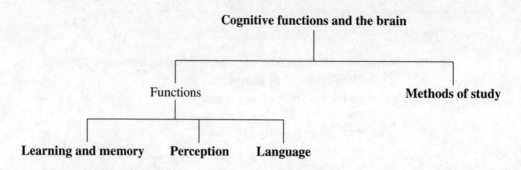

Cognitive functions and the brain

Functions **Methods of study**

Learning and memory **Perception** **Language**

Each of those segments can then be subdivided into smaller tree diagrams. These can be useful in helping you to structure your revision.

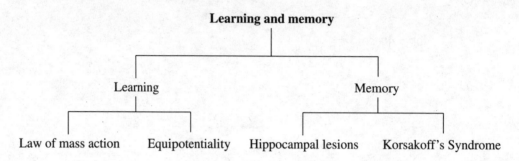

Learning and memory

Learning Memory

Law of mass action Equipotentiality Hippocampal lesions Korsakoff's Syndrome

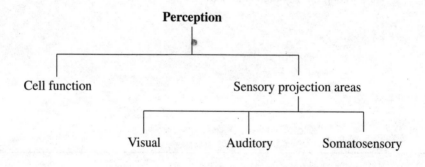

Perception

Cell function Sensory projection areas

Visual Auditory Somatosensory

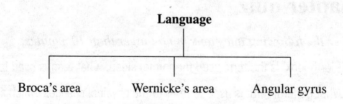

Language

Broca's area Wernicke's area Angular gyrus

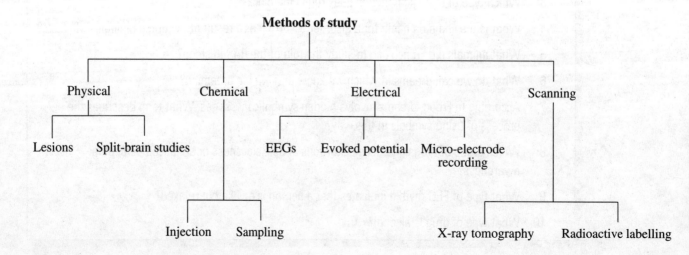

Methods of study

Physical Chemical Electrical Scanning

Lesions Split-brain studies EEGs Evoked potential Micro-electrode recording

Injection Sampling X-ray tomography Radioactive labelling

Planning an essay

When you are planning an essay for an examination, remember that you won't have enough time to write down everything you know about the subject. This means that the essay's structure is particularly important. You must bring in as much information that is relevant to the question as you can, and leave out extra or irrelevant details.

Even writing quite quickly, you will probably be able to write only one paragraph in five minutes. So your essay structure must be matched to the time you have available and you should plan what the paragraphs will cover with that in mind. Using this method, a 45-minute essay involves five minutes' thinking time and produces eight paragraphs. For example:

SAMPLE QUESTION

Discuss the question of localisation of function in the cerebral cortex.

Paragraph 1	introduction: cerebrum as dominant structure in human brain
Paragraph 2	sensory areas
Paragraph 3	motor cortex and its arrangement
Paragraph 4	links with other brain structures for movement/sensation
Paragraph 5	language areas
Paragraph 6	split-brain studies
Paragraph 7	learning and memory: equipotentiality
Paragraph 8	conclusion: some functions localised, 'higher' functions not

Of course, this isn't the only way of tackling this essay. There are several other possibilities. Try producing some essay outlines for yourself, using the following questions:

1 *What do psychologists know about links between the brain, learning and memory?*
2 *Outline and discuss brain mechanisms of perception and movement.*
3 *Giving examples, discuss how psychologists have gone about studying the human brain.*
4 *How does the brain process spoken and written language?*

Question 1: *What do psychologists know about links between the brain, learning and memory?*

Paragraph 1	introduction:
Paragraph 2	
Paragraph 3	
Paragraph 4	
Paragraph 5	
Paragraph 6	
Paragraph 7	
Paragraph 8	conclusion:

Question 2: *Outline and discuss brain mechanisms of perception and movement.*

Paragraph 1	introduction:
Paragraph 2	
Paragraph 3	

Paragraph 4

Paragraph 5

Paragraph 6

Paragraph 7

Paragraph 8   conclusion:

Question 3:   *Giving examples, discuss how psychologists have gone about studying the human brain.*

Paragraph 1   introduction:

Paragraph 2

Paragraph 3

Paragraph 4

Paragraph 5

Paragraph 6

Paragraph 7

Paragraph 8   conclusion:

Question 4:   *How does the brain process spoken and written language?*

Paragraph 1   introduction:

Paragraph 2

Paragraph 3

Paragraph 4

Paragraph 5

Paragraph 6

Paragraph 7

Paragraph 8   conclusion:

Chapter summary

(*Psychology: an Introduction*, page 139)

1   The cerebrum seems to be involved in a wide variety of cognitive functions. Memory is usually a cerebral function, but the hippocampus of the limbic system may also be involved.

2   Sense perception appears to operate in the sensory projection areas of the cerebral cortex. Vision, touch, smell and hearing all have specific areas on the cerebrum.

3   There are three specific areas for language on the cerebrum. These are Broca's area, Wernicke's area, and the angular gyrus. Each area is concerned with a different aspect of language functioning.

4   Learning does not seem to be a localised cerebral function. The cerebrum seems to operate on the basis of equipotentiality – the whole of the cortex seems to be equally important in learning.

5   Sperry showed that the halves of the cerebrum can operate as separate 'brains' if they are divided surgically. The left side deals more with language and logic, while the right side seems to deal more with creative pursuits.

Key sections for revision

1   the brain and memory
2   sensory perception
3   language areas
4   learning
5   methods of studying the brain
6   split-brain studies

Issues and perspectives

Using the following table, note down any features of interest which relate to the key sections of the chapter.

Key section	Methods of study	Evaluation and criticism	Ethical issues
1 the brain and memory			
2 sensory perception			
3 language areas			
4 learning			
5 methods of studying the brain			
6 split-brain studies			

Revision questions

Short-answer questions are useful for testing your knowledge of an area while you are revising, and for making sure that you understand it. They also often appear in examinations, and when they do you will have only a limited amount of time to answer them. The questions will be marked according to the information you have used to answer them and what you can attain marks for will be set out in a mark scheme.

Here are two 10-mark questions, with typical marking schemes which an examiner might use to assess answers.

Describe the main methods used to study the functions of the brain.

physical methods	(up to)	2 marks
chemical methods	(up to)	2 marks
electrical methods	(up to)	3 marks
scanning	(up to)	3 marks
		Total 10 marks

Describe and discuss a typical 'split-brain' study.

structure/function of corpus callosum	(up to)	2 marks
description of study	(up to)	3 marks
outcome of study	(up to)	3 marks
implications of study	(up to)	2 marks
		Total 10 marks

As you can see, each question has its own mark scheme and these share out the marks between the different types of knowledge needed to answer the question.

Bearing this in mind, try to work out your own mark schemes for each of the following questions. Each question is worth 10 marks. If you feel that you need more help, look at the mark schemes in the other chapters.

1   *Critically evaluate the use of 'split-brain' studies to investigate hemisphere functioning.*

2   *What parts of the cerebral cortex are involved in reading aloud, and what does each part do?*

3   *Describe Lashley's study of learning and the cerebral cortex.*

4   *Outline and discuss <u>two</u> ways in which damage to the brain can influence memory.*

5   *What did Hubel and Wiesel discover about visual information processing?*

When you have written your mark scheme, turn to the relevant pages in your textbook and make sure that your scheme reflects the information covered by that topic.

Answering revision questions

Now try answering each of these questions, giving yourself 15 minutes to complete each one. At the end of that time, mark your answer, using the mark scheme that you have developed.

(NB: It is essential that you write the mark scheme <u>before</u> you try to answer the question! Doing it the other way round would be completely pointless because you would be too influenced by what you have already written.)

1   *Critically evaluate the use of 'split-brain' studies to investigate hemisphere functioning.*

2   *What parts of the cerebral cortex are involved in reading aloud, and what does each part do?*

3   *Describe Lashley's study of learning and the cerebral cortex.*

4   *Outline and discuss two ways in which damage to the brain can influence memory.*

5   *What did Hubel and Wiesel discover about visual information processing?*

A suggestion for practical work

This study has been derived from Exercise 8.2 suggested on page 135 of *Psychology: an Introduction*. It is an experiment which will allow you to investigate cerebral dominance and learning a new physical skill.

You will need to conduct the experiment with several people. Remember that the important variable is not left or right hand, but whether it is their preferred or non-preferred hand.

Carrying out the study

In planning your study, you will need to identify the following (consult Chapter 22, pages 424–8 of *Psychology: an Introduction* if you need further explanation):

hypothesis _____

null hypothesis _____

independent variable _____

dependent variable _____

design _____

controls _____

ethical considerations _____

_____

_____

_____

_____

Make notes on how you will carry out this experiment. _____

_____

_____

_____

_____

Analysing the results

You will need a summary table of results which includes the mean, median and mode for your two sets of scores. It should be called Table 1 and will need a title telling your reader exactly what it is about. Use Appendix 2A (page 205) to help you in drawing up your table.

You will also need a diagram to display your findings visually. This will be called Fig. 1. In this instance, you should draw a bar chart, comparing the mean scores for preferred hands and non-preferred hands. Use the notes in Appendix 2B (page 205) to help you to draw your bar chart.

Reporting the study

You are now ready to write up your experiment in the correct format.

Use Checklist A in the Appendix (page 210) to make sure you have included everything you need to.

Sample examination questions

Midlands Examining Group,   June 1990
Physiological Module, Source C, Questions 12/16
Paper reference: 754

Split Brain Patients

W.J. was a war veteran who suffered from severe epilepsy which could not be controlled. The doctors decided to cut the corpus callosum which connects the two hemispheres of the brain. This operation stops the spread of seizures from one hemisphere to the other. W.J.'s operation was an immediate success in that his seizures were drastically reduced and there appeared to be little effect on his behaviour. He was still able to perform intellectual tasks and work normally. However, careful testing showed that the operation had some interesting side effects. W.J. was given a set of black and white blocks and asked to copy a pattern with his left hand. He could do this successfully. It should have been easy for him to do the same patterns with the other hand since he had just watched himself do it. However, W.J. had great difficulty with his right hand and was unable to copy the pattern.

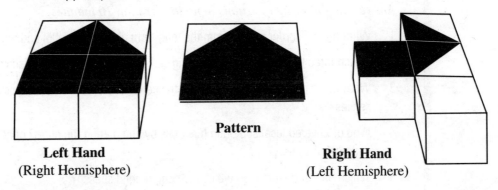

Left Hand
(Right Hemisphere)

Pattern

Right Hand
(Left Hemisphere)

W.J. seemed distressed that he was unable to copy the pattern and amazingly enough his left hand seemed distressed as well, as it tried several times to correct the right hand's efforts to complete the pattern. The explanation for this effect is based on the localisation of function in the brain. Spatial ability and drawing are located in the right hemisphere of the brain.

[adapted from Ornstein and Thompson, *The Amazing Brain*]

12 What is the *corpus callosum*?

_____ [1]

13 Why was W.J. able to complete the pattern with his left hand?

_____

_____ [2]

14 (a) What is meant by the term *localisation of function*?

_____

_____ [2]

    (b) Name another area of the brain that has a localised function.

_____ [1]

15 Give TWO other difficulties that a split brain patient might have.

_____

_____ [2]

16   Describe some of the other ways that psychologists have tried to investigate the brain.

_____

_____

_____

_____

_____

_____

_____

_____   [8]

Chapter quiz

Answer the following questions in no longer than 10 minutes:

1   What brain disorder results from the long-term abuse of alcohol and inadequate nutrition?

2   Which three types of visual processing cell did Hubel and Wiesel discover?

3   What name is given to the regions of the cerebral cortex which process information from the senses?

4   Who discovered localised brain functions by stimulating the cortex of conscious patients undergoing surgery?

5   Which part of the brain do we use to comprehend speech?

6   What is the technical term for severing connections in the brain?

7   What operation did Gooch's patients experience?

8   What name is given to Lashley's discovery that one part of the association cortex seems to be much the same as another in its overall functioning?

9   The four main ways of studying brain function are physical, chemical, electrical and ?

10   What disorder were split-brain operations performed to alleviate?

Chapter 9 – Thinking and problem-solving

This chapter can be divided into four major segments, as follows:

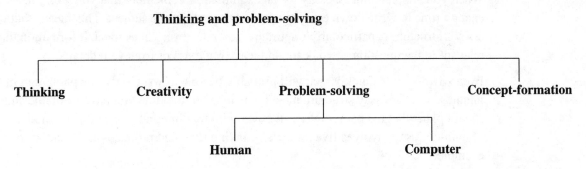

Each of those segments can then be subdivided into smaller tree diagrams. These can be useful in helping you to structure your revision.

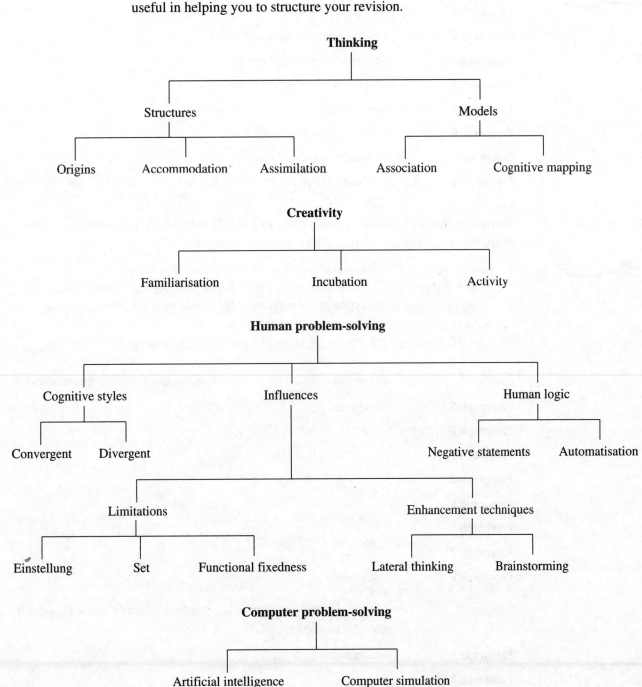

Planning an essay

When you are planning an essay for an examination, remember that you won't have enough time to write down everything you know about the subject. This means that the essay's structure is particularly important. You must bring in as much information that is relevant to the question as you can, and leave out extra or irrelevant details.

Even writing quite quickly, you will probably be able to write only one paragraph in five minutes, so your essay structure must be matched to the time you have available and you should plan what the paragraphs will cover with that in mind. Using this method, a 45-minute essay involves five minutes' thinking time and produces eight paragraphs. For example:

SAMPLE QUESTION

Discuss some of the factors that can aid or inhibit problem-solving and reasoning.

Paragraph 1	introduction: day-to-day uses of problem-solving
Paragraph 2	trial-and-error, experience and insight
Paragraph 3	functional fixedness/Einstellung
Paragraph 4	lateral thinking and brainstorming
Paragraph 5	cognitive style
Paragraph 6	human logic: negative statements
Paragraph 7	automatism: the Stroop effect
Paragraph 8	conclusion: habits/assumptions are powerful influences that may be either helpful or not helpful

Of course, this isn't the only possible way to tackle this question. Try producing some essay outlines for yourself, using the following questions:

QUESTIONS

1 *Outline and discuss some of the major theories of thinking and creativity.*
2 *How might our experiences or assumptions influence how we approach problem-solving?*
3 *Giving evidence, discuss some of the differences between human and computer-based reasoning.*
4 *What is a concept? What do we know about human concept-formation?*

Question 1:	*Outline and discuss some of the major theories of thinking and creativity.*
Paragraph 1	introduction:
Paragraph 2	
Paragraph 3	
Paragraph 4	
Paragraph 5	
Paragraph 6	
Paragraph 7	
Paragraph 8	conclusion:
Question 2:	*How might our experiences or assumptions influence how we approach problem-solving?*
Paragraph 1	introduction:
Paragraph 2	
Paragraph 3	
Paragraph 4	

Paragraph 5

Paragraph 6

Paragraph 7

Paragraph 8   conclusion:

Question 3:   *Giving evidence, discuss some of the differences between human and computer-based reasoning.*

Paragraph 1   introduction:

Paragraph 2

Paragraph 3

Paragraph 4

Paragraph 5

Paragraph 6

Paragraph 7

Paragraph 8   conclusion:

Question 4:   *What is a concept? What do we know about human concept-formation?*

Paragraph 1   introduction:

Paragraph 2

Paragraph 3

Paragraph 4

Paragraph 5

Paragraph 6

Paragraph 7

Paragraph 8   conclusion:

Chapter summary

(*Psychology: an Introduction*, page 165)

1   Thinking can be defined as 'the internal representation of events'. Psychologists have seen the origins of thought in different ways: Freud saw it as goal-oriented; Piaget saw it as adaptation; and Dewey saw it as arising from discrepancies.

2   Very creative people seem to show a three-stage process to their work: familiarisation incubation and activity.

3   Two main mechanisms of learning to solve problems are trial and error learning and insight learning.

4   Work on cognitive styles has shown that people may be either convergent or divergent thinkers and that this may affect their success in school. Another aspect of cognitive style is lateral thinking, which involves looking for unusual approaches to problems.

5   Work on human problem-solving has looked at learning sets, functional fixedness and Einstellung. Wason showed that human logic could differ from formal logic, and the Stroop effect shows how we use automatic routines in our thinking.

6   Various models of thinking have been developed: associationist, cognitive maps and computer models.

7   Work on concept-formation has shown that people use different strategies to identify concepts. Piaget argued that concept-formation occurred through the formation of schemata.

Key sections for revision

1   origins of thinking
2   creativity
3   mechanisms of learning
4   cognitive style
5   problem-solving
6   models of thinking
7   concept-formation

Issues and perspectives

Using the following table, note down any features of interest which relate to the key sections of the chapter.

Key section	Methods of study	Evaluation and criticism	Ethical issues
1 origins of thinking			
2 creativity			
3 mechanisms of learning			
4 cognitive style			
5 problem-solving			
6 models of thinking			
7 concept-formation			

Revision questions

Short-answer questions are useful for testing your knowledge of an area while you are revising, and for making sure that you understand it. They also often appear in examinations, and when they do you will have only a limited amount of time to answer them. The questions will be marked according to the information you have used to answer them and what you can attain marks for will be set out in a mark scheme.

Here are two 10-mark questions, with typical marking schemes which an examiner might use to assess answers.

Discuss the views of any <u>two</u> of the following on the process of thinking: Tolman, Dewey, Locke, Piaget.

description of theory (3 marks each)	(up to)	6 marks
evaluation/implication (2 marks each)	(up to)	4 marks
	(any one theorist max. 5 marks)	
	Total 10 marks	

Describe Collins and Quillian's study of concept-formation.

description of study	(up to)	4 marks
outcome of study	(up to)	3 marks
implications of study	(up to)	3 marks
	Total 10 marks	

As you can see, each question has its own mark scheme and these share out the marks between the different types of knowledge needed to answer the question.

Bearing this in mind, try to work out your own mark schemes for each of the following questions. Each question is worth 10 marks. If you feel that you need more help, look at the mark schemes in the other chapters.

1   *Using an example, describe the three phases of creativity.*

2   *Describe and critically evaluate computer simulations of problem-solving.*

3   *Outline <u>two</u> methods of improving human problem-solving.*

4   *What did the Gestalt psychologists discover about human problem-solving?*

5   *Using Wason's findings, distinguish between human reasoning and computer logic.*

When you have written your mark scheme, turn to the relevant pages in your textbook and make sure that your scheme reflects the information covered by that topic.

Answering revision questions

Now try answering each of these questions, giving yourself 15 minutes to complete each one. At the end of that time, mark your answer, using the mark scheme that you have developed.

(NB: It is essential that you write the mark scheme <u>before</u> you try to answer the question! Doing it the other way round would be completely pointless because you would be too influenced by what you have already written.)

 **QUESTIONS**

1   Using an example, describe the three phases of creativity.

2   Describe and critically evaluate computer simulations of problem-solving.

3   Outline <u>two</u> methods of improving human problem-solving.

4   What did the Gestalt psychologists discover about human problem-solving?

5   Using Wason's findings, distinguish between human reasoning and computer logic.

A suggestion for practical work

This study has been derived from Exercise 9.1 suggested on page 154 of *Psychology: an Introduction*. It is an experiment which will allow you to investigate risky-shift processes.

After taking individual scores and then reaching a group decision, ask each person to do the individual test again. This will give you a set of scores for comparison.

Carrying out the study

STUDY

In planning your study, you will need to identify the following (consult Chapter 22, pages 424–8 of *Psychology: an Introduction* if you need further explanation):

hypothesis _____

null hypothesis _____

independent variable _____

dependent variable _____

controls _____

design _____

ethical considerations _____

_____

_____

_____

_____

Make notes on how you will carry out this study. _____

_____

_____

_____

_____

Analysing the results

You will need a summary table of results which includes the mean, median and mode for your two groups. It should be called Table 1 and will need a title telling your reader exactly what it is about. Look in Appendix 2A (page 205) for guidance in drawing up a table.

You will also need a diagram to display your findings visually. This will be called Fig. 1. Use the notes in Appendix 2B (page 205) to help you.

In this instance, you will need a bar chart showing the mean scores from the two conditions: before the group discussion, and afterwards.

Reporting the study

You are now ready to write up your experiment in the correct format.

Use Checklist A in the Appendix (page 210) to make sure you have included everything you need to.

Sample examination questions

Midlands Examining Group, June 1994
Cognitive Module, Source B, Questions 6/8
Paper reference: 500

Problem-solving – swinging for a solution

A problem-solving task is illustrated below.

The task is to tie the two strings together. If you hold one, the other is out of reach. The scissors and the stapler on the floor can be used.

Most people keep on trying to reach the string until eventually they give up. The solution is to use the scissors or stapler as a weight, so that you can swing one of the strings towards you.

The reason that many people do not think of doing this is because they can only think of the everyday use for scissors and staplers. Their thinking has become rigid – they cannot think how to use a familiar object in an unfamiliar way. This is called **functional fixedness.**

6   According to the text, what is *functional fixedness*?

_____ [1]

7   (a)   Some people solve the problem easily. Suggest **one** possible reason why one person might be better at solving the string problem than another person.

_____

_____ [2]

     (b)   Functional fixedness makes problem-solving more difficult. Describe **one other** factor which can **limit** problem-solving ability.

_____

_____

_____ [3]

8   (a)   **Divergent thinking** involves thinking in a creative way about a problem. How does divergent thinking differ from *convergent* thinking?

_____

_____ [2]

     (b)   Give an example from everyday life when *divergent thinking* is useful.

_____

_____ [1]

Chapter quiz

Answer the following questions in no longer than 10 minutes:

1   Who developed the 'trouble theory' of thought?

2   What is the second stage of creativity, according to Wallas and Ghiselin?

3   What apparatus did Thorndike use to study learning?

4   What name do we give to a sudden flash of insight in solving problems?

5   What type of problem-solving did de Bono make famous?

6   What do we call it when someone is unable to think of a use for an object other than the one for which it was originally made?

7   What name is given to the steps involved in solving a problem?

8   Which philosopher is closely linked with the model of thinking known as associationism?

9   What do we call attempts to replicate human problem-solving using computers?

10 What aspect of their participants' behaviour did Collins and Quillian measure when they investigated hierarchical concept storage?

Chapter 10 – Language

This chapter can be divided into three major segments, as follows:

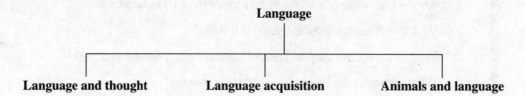

Each of those segments can then be subdivided into smaller tree diagrams. These can be useful in helping you to structure your revision.

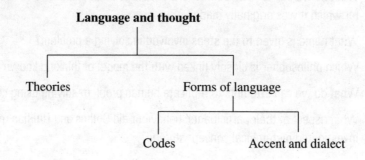

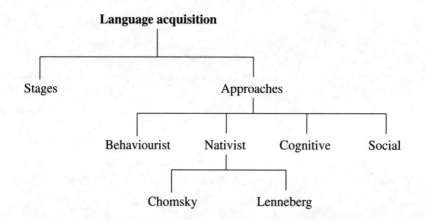

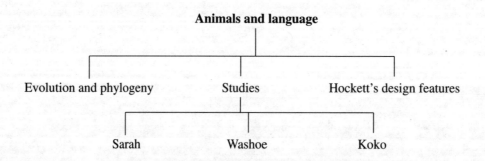

Planning an essay

When you are planning an essay for an examination, remember that you won't have enough time to write down everything you know about the subject. This means that the essay's structure is particularly important. You must bring in as much information that is relevant to the question as you can, and leave out extra or irrelevant details.

Even writing quite quickly, you will probably be able to write only one paragraph in five minutes, so your essay structure must be matched to the time you have available and you should plan what the paragraphs will cover with that in mind. Using this method, a 45-minute essay involves five minutes' thinking time and produces eight paragraphs. For example:

SAMPLE QUESTION

How does a child learn to talk?

Paragraph 1	introduction: rapidity of infant language acquisition
Paragraph 2	stages of language competence
Paragraph 3	behaviourist explanation: Skinner
Paragraph 4	nativist explanation: Chomsky
Paragraph 5	critical period: Lenneberg
Paragraph 6	social influences: Genie
Paragraph 7	human interaction as 'teaching' child
Paragraph 8	conclusion: language learning as a social process

Of course, this isn't the only possible way of answering this question: it's just an example. Now try producing some essay outlines for yourself, using the following questions:

QUESTIONS

1   *Is it true that the language that we use determines how we think? Give evidence for your answer.*
2   *What factors are thought to influence language acquisition in children?*
3   *Discuss the idea that children use special forms of grammar while they are acquiring language.*
4   *What evidence is there for the idea that animals could be taught to use human language?*

Question 1:   *Is it true that the language that we use determines how we think? Give evidence for your answer.*

Paragraph 1	introduction:
Paragraph 2	
Paragraph 3	
Paragraph 4	
Paragraph 5	
Paragraph 6	
Paragraph 7	
Paragraph 8	conclusion:

Question 2:   *What factors are thought to influence language acquisition in children?*

Paragraph 1	introduction:
Paragraph 2	
Paragraph 3	
Paragraph 4	
Paragraph 5	

Paragraph 6

Paragraph 7

Paragraph 8   conclusion:

Question 3:   *Discuss the idea that children use special forms of grammar while they are acquiring language.*

Paragraph 1   introduction:

Paragraph 2

Paragraph 3

Paragraph 4

Paragraph 5

Paragraph 6

Paragraph 7

Paragraph 8   conclusion:

Question 4:   *Is there evidence that animals could be taught to use human language?*

Paragraph 1   introduction:

Paragraph 2

Paragraph 3

Paragraph 4

Paragraph 5

Paragraph 6

Paragraph 7

Paragraph 8   conclusion:

Chapter summary

(*Psychology: an Introduction*, page 186)

1   The relationship between language and thought has been seen in different ways: thought as sub-vocal behaviour; thought as dependent on language; and language as a tool of thought.

2   Bernstein identified elaborated and restricted codes of language, and argued that working-class people could use only restricted codes. Labov and others showed that this was not the case, but that social expectation may have an influence on development.

3   Children go through identifiable stages as they acquire language, which have been studied by Brown and other psychologists.

4   The behaviourist view of language acquisition was put forward by Skinner, who said it happened through operant conditioning of the child's babbling.

5   Chomsky and Lenneberg put forward nativist theories of language acquisition. Chomsky proposed an innate Language Acquisition Device (LAD), and Lenneberg said there was a critical period.

6   Social theories of language acquisition have emphasised the need for human interaction which children have when they are learning language.

7   J. and P. de Villiers showed how parents teach their children language naturally, through 'baby talk', expansion of the child's utterances and other devices.

8   Studies of animals learning language have shown that apes may be able to learn to use simple language but not as easily as human children can.

Key sections for revision

1 language and thinking
2 elaborated/restricted codes
3 stages of language acquisition
4 language as conditioning
5 language as innate
6 language as social interaction
7 animals and language

Issues and perspectives

Using the following table, note down any features of interest which relate to the key sections of the chapter.

Key section	Methods of study	Evaluation and criticism	Ethical issues
1 language and thinking			
2 elaborated/restricted codes			
3 stages of language acquisition			
4 language as conditioning			
5 language as innate			
6 language as social interaction			
7 animals and language			

Revision questions

Short-answer questions are useful for testing your knowledge of an area while you are revising, and for making sure that you understand it. They also often appear in examinations, and when they do you will have only a limited amount of time to answer them. The questions will be marked according to the information you have used to answer them and what you can attain marks for will be set out in a mark scheme.

Here are two 10-mark questions, with typical marking schemes which an examiner might use to assess answers.

Distinguish between elaborated and restricted codes of language.

origins: linguistic relativity	(up to)	2 marks
description of restricted code	(up to)	2 marks
description of elaborated code	(up to)	2 marks
comparison and evaluation	(up to)	4 marks
		Total 10 marks

How did Skinner explain language acquisition?

behaviourist approach	(up to)	2 marks
babbling and adult reaction	(up to)	3 marks
reinforcement and shaping	(up to)	3 marks
generalisation/discrimination	(up to)	2 marks
		Total 10 marks

As you can see, each question has its own mark scheme and these share out the marks between the different types of knowledge needed to answer the question.

Bearing this in mind, try to work out your own mark schemes for each of the following questions. Each question is worth 10 marks. If you feel that you need more help, look at the mark schemes in the other chapters.

1   *What did Piaget think about the relationship between language and thought?*

2   *What were the five stages of language acquisition identified by Brown?*

3   *Outline the nativist views of language acquisition put forward by Chomsky and Lenneberg.*

4   *Describe <u>two</u> ways that parental interaction helps a child to learn language.*

5   *Describe and discuss <u>one</u> study of apes learning human language.*

When you have written your mark scheme, turn to the relevant pages in your textbook and make sure that your scheme reflects the information covered by that topic.

Answering revision questions

Now try answering each of these questions, giving yourself 15 minutes to complete each one. At the end of that time, mark your answer, using the mark scheme that you have developed.

(NB: It is essential that you write the mark scheme <u>before</u> you try to answer the question! Doing it the other way round would be completely pointless because you would be too influenced by what you have already written.)

QUESTIONS

1   *What did Piaget think about the relationship between language and thought?*

2   *What were the five stages of language acquisition identified by Brown?*

3   *Outline the nativist views of language acquisition put forward by Chomsky and Lenneberg.*

4   *Describe two ways that parental interaction helps a child to learn language.*

5   *Describe and discuss one study of apes learning human language.*

A suggestion for practical work

This study has been derived from exercise 10.1 suggested on pages 167–8 of *Psychology: an Introduction*.

This is a correlation study, allowing you to compare ratings of how commonly items are used, with how many words there are for them.

Begin by making a list of ten common and not-so-common types of items and then ask people to rank them in order of frequency. Next, ask people to do the 'alien' game described in the chapter. You can correlate the rank order of the term on the list with the number of words that people could think of.

Carrying out the study

In planning your study, you will need to identify the following (consult Chapter 22, pages 424–8 of *Psychology: an Introduction* if you need further explanation):

hypothesis _____

null hypothesis _____

variable 1 _____

variable 2 _____

controls _____

ethical considerations _____

_____

_____

_____

_____

_____

Make notes on how you will carry out this study. _____

_____

_____

_____

_____

_____

Analysing the results

You will need to draw up a scattergram to show the relationship between your two variables. Use the notes in Appendix 2C (page 207) to help you to do this.

Reporting the study

You are now ready to write up your experiment in the correct format.

Use Checklist B in the Appendix (page 210) to make sure you have included everything you need to.

Sample examination question

Reading 4.10   Language development

Trevarthen (1974) studied babies from birth to six months with the aid of recording devices. He noted a particular kind of behaviour in babies as young as six weeks which he termed 'pre-speech'. This is a primitive attempt at speech by moving the lips and tongue, sometimes vocally, at other times soundlessly. He noted also that as early as two months, babies make soft, low vowel sounds in response to others. This responsive vocalisation may be the beginning of 'taking turns' as babies and adults do in conversation later on.

In a longitudinal study lasting 10 years, Roger Brown used naturalistic observation techniques to study the development of language in three children, Adam, Eve and Sarah. The children were visited in their homes and tape recordings made of conversations between child and mother. The tape recordings were later transcribed and analysed by Brown and colleagues. The following are among the insights obtained from Brown's work.

1   Early sentences produced by young children are short and incomplete grammatically. However, the words retained are 'telegraphic' in that they preserve the meaning of the message, while the smaller 'functor' words, which are not essential to the meaning, are left out, e.g. 'baby highchair', meaning 'baby is in the highchair'. Correct word order is invariably retained.

2   Children up to the age of four/five have difficulty in correctly expressing negation (I will not walk), past tenses (I shouted), plurals (give me the sweets).

3   Early sentences are much the same whatever language the child speaks. Whether the child is learning English, Russian or Chinese, she/he expresses the same variety of meanings, e.g. statements about location ('spoon table'), possession ('my doll') actions ('Mummy dance').

Brown's innovatory approach to the study of language acquisition has produced a vast amount of data which has provided material for many further studies. However, the study has its limitations. Because of the nature and size of the sample, it is difficult to generalise findings to all children. Also, child speech was analysed from a typed transcript of the recordings. It was noted by Robinson (1981) that features of the language used, such as intonation, pitch and stress were not included, and the caretaker's utterances and the context in which the utterances were made were often left out.

Cazden (1965) found that a group of children whose utterances were commented upon on a regular basis over a period of three months showed more progress in language development than a similar group whose utterances were expanded upon and imitation of correct language encouraged.

A. Birch and T. Malim (1988) *Developmental Psychology* Intertext

1   What is meant by 'pre-speech'?

_____

_____ [2]

2   Describe **two** differences that Brown found between the language of young children and adults.

_____

_____

_____ [4]

3   Report Cazden's (1965) findings in your own words.

_____

_____

[4]

4   Discuss Brown's theory on the social aspects of language development.

_____

_____

[6]

Chapter quiz

Answer the following questions in no longer than 10 minutes:

1   Which hypothesis involves the idea that thinking depends on language?

2   What, according to Piaget, is the distinctive characteristic of the young child's speech?

3   What other function of the young child's speech, apart from the communicative function, was identified by Vygotsky?

4   What type of language code is used by middle-class people, according to Bernstein?

5   What name is given to Brown's theory of infant grammar?

6   What term means the basic units of sound involved in spoken language?

7   What innate structure for language learning was proposed by the linguist Noam Chomsky?

8   What aspect of human experience do modern theories of language acquisition emphasise?

9   What is the name given to a system used for placing animals in an evolutionary sequence, according to how 'advanced' each one appears to be?

10   What type of animal was studied by Patterson?

This chapter can be divided into four major segments, as follows:

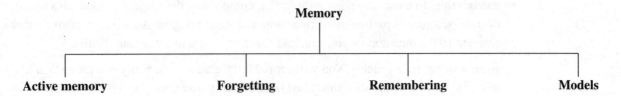

Memory

Active memory   **Forgetting**   **Remembering**   **Models**

Each of those segments can then be subdivided into smaller tree diagrams. These can be useful in helping you to structure your revision.

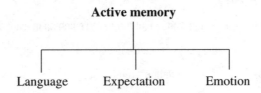

Active memory

Language   Expectation   Emotion

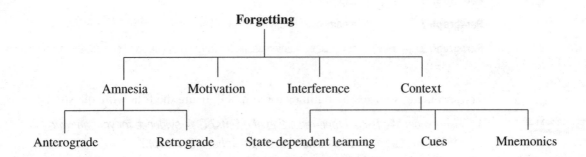

Forgetting

Amnesia   Motivation   Interference   Context

Anterograde   Retrograde   State-dependent learning   Cues   Mnemonics

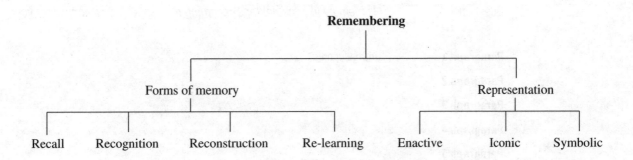

Remembering

Forms of memory   Representation

Recall   Recognition   Reconstruction   Re-learning   Enactive   Iconic   Symbolic

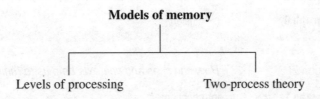

Models of memory

Levels of processing   Two-process theory

Planning an essay

When you are planning an essay for an examination, remember that you won't have enough time to write down everything you know about the subject. This means that the essay's structure is particularly important. You must bring in as much information that is relevant to the question as you can, and leave out extra or irrelevant details.

Even writing quite quickly, you will probably be able to write only one paragraph in five minutes, so your essay structure must be matched to the time you have available and you should plan what the paragraphs will cover with that in mind. Using this method, a 45-minute essay involves five minutes' thinking time and produces eight paragraphs. For example:

Why do we forget?

Paragraph 1	introduction: forgetting common in everyday life
Paragraph 2	physical causes: amnesia
Paragraph 3	motivation: Freud, moods
Paragraph 4	interference: proactive or retroactive
Paragraph 5	context: external or internal (state-dependent)
Paragraph 6	lack of cues
Paragraph 7	mnemonics: finding cues to aid memory
Paragraph 8	conclusion: many reasons for forgetting; cues and context the most common

Try producing some essay outlines for yourself, using the following questions:

1   *Is memory like factual tape-recording of events? Give evidence for your answer.*
2   *How can cues and contexts help us to remember information?*
3   *Discuss the use of imagery in remembering.*
4   *Compare two different models of memory processing.*

Question 1:	*Is memory like factual tape-recording of events? Give evidence for your answer.*
Paragraph 1	introduction:
Paragraph 2	
Paragraph 3	
Paragraph 4	
Paragraph 5	
Paragraph 6	
Paragraph 7	
Paragraph 8	conclusion:

Question 2:	*How can cues and contexts help us to remember information?*
Paragraph 1	introduction:
Paragraph 2	
Paragraph 3	
Paragraph 4	

Paragraph 5

Paragraph 6

Paragraph 7

Paragraph 8   conclusion:

Question 3:   *Discuss the use of imagery in remembering.*

Paragraph 1   introduction:

Paragraph 2

Paragraph 3

Paragraph 4

Paragraph 5

Paragraph 6

Paragraph 7

Paragraph 8   conclusion:

Question 4:   *Compare two different models of memory processing.*

Paragraph 1   introduction:

Paragraph 2

Paragraph 3

Paragraph 4

Paragraph 5

Paragraph 6

Paragraph 7

Paragraph 8   conclusion:

Chapter summary

(*Psychology: an Introduction*, page 202)

1 Memory is an active process which can be affected by factors like language and expectation.
2 Bartlett showed that we make an 'effort after meaning' in which we try to fit our memories into the existing schemata that we hold.
3 Many theories have been put forward to explain forgetting, ranging from brain damage or disease, through repression, interference, and state-dependent learning, to lack of context and cues for recall.
4 Ebbinghaus identified four ways of remembering: recall, recognition, reconstruction and re-learning savings.
5 Our use of imagery in memory may change as we grow older. Revision techniques involving imagery can be highly successful in improving memory.
6 Craik and Lockart developed the levels of processing approach to memory, which argued that apparent differences between long- and short-term memory arose as a result of less-thorough coding or processing of the information to be remembered.

Key sections for revision

1 memory as an active process
2 adjusting memories
3 forgetting
4 forms of remembering
5 imagery
6 theories of memory

Issues and perspective

Using the following table, note down any features of interest which relate to the key sections of the chapter.

Key section	Methods of study	Evaluation and criticism	Ethical issues
1 memory as an active process			
2 adjusting memories			
3 forgetting			
4 forms of remembering			
5 imagery			
6 theories of memory			

Revision questions

Short-answer questions are useful for testing your knowledge of an area while you are revising, and for making sure that you understand it. They also often appear in examinations, and when they do you will have only a limited amount of time to answer them. The questions will be marked according to the information you have used to answer them and what you can attain marks for will be set out in a mark scheme.

Here are two 10-mark questions, with typical marking schemes which an examiner might use to assess answers.

Outline two ways that imagery can be used to aid remembering.

definition, iconic representation, etc.	(up to)	2 marks
method 1	(up to)	3 marks
method 2	(up to)	3 marks
examples/applications	(up to)	2 marks
		Total 10 marks

What is state-dependent learning?

context as factor in recall	(up to)	2 marks
definition/explanation	(up to)	3 marks
example/study	(up to)	3 marks
implications	(up to)	2 marks
		Total 10 marks

As you can see, each question has its own mark scheme and these share out the marks between the different types of knowledge needed to answer the question.

Bearing this in mind, try to work out your own mark schemes for each of the following questions. Each question is worth 10 marks. If you feel that you need more help, look at the mark schemes in the other chapters.

1   *Describe and discuss a study of memory as an active process.*

2   *How does what Bartlett called 'effort after meaning' affect how we remember information?*

3   *List the major explanations for forgetting.*

4   *Briefly describe Ebbinghaus's research methods and major findings about memory.*

5   *How does the levels of processing approach differ from the two-process theory of memory?*

When you have written your mark scheme, turn to the relevant pages in your textbook and make sure that your scheme reflects the information covered by that topic.

Answering revision questions

Now try answering each of these questions, giving yourself 15 minutes to complete each one. At the end of that time, mark your answer, using the mark scheme that you have developed.

(NB: It is essential that you write the mark scheme <u>before</u> you try to answer the question! Doing it the other way round would be completely pointless because you would be too influenced by what you have already written.)

QUESTIONS

1 *Describe and discuss a study of memory as an active process.*

2 *How does what Bartlett called 'effort after meaning' affect how we remember information?*

3 *List the major explanations for forgetting.*

4 *Briefly describe Ebbinghaus's research methods and major findings about memory.*

5 *How does the levels of processing approach differ from the two-process theory of memory?*

A suggestion for practical work

This study has been derived from Exercise 11.2 suggested on page 199 of *Psychology: an Introduction*. It is a correlation, allowing you to explore the relationship between levels of processing and the amount you can recall.

You will need to begin by identifying five different revision tasks which require different degrees of processing. As an example, you might go from mental repetition, to copying the information out, to reading it aloud, to summarising it and to making it into a diagram (like the tree diagrams at the beginning of this chapter). Ask people to use these methods to go over the material and then test them to see how much they remember.

Carrying out the study

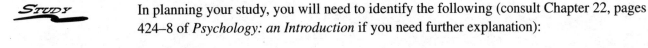

In planning your study, you will need to identify the following (consult Chapter 22, pages 424–8 of *Psychology: an Introduction* if you need further explanation):

hypothesis _____

null hypothesis _____

variable 1 _____

variable 2 _____

controls _____

ethical considerations _____

_____

_____

_____

_____

Make notes on how you will carry out this study. _____

_____

_____

_____

_____

Analysing the results

You will need to draw up a scattergram to show the relationship between your two variables. Use the notes in Appendix 2D (page 208) to help you to do this.

Reporting the study

You are now ready to write up your experiment in the correct format.

Use Checklist B in the Appendix (page 210) to make sure you have included everything you need to.

Sample examination question

Northern Examining Association, June 1990
Paper 2, Question 2
Paper reference: 2175

2   The flow diagram below represents three stages of memory.

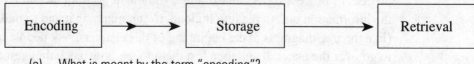

| Encoding | → | Storage | → | Retrieval |

(a)   What is meant by the term "encoding"?

_____

_____

_____   [3]

(b)

The Spanish word for tent is "carpa". The picture above is part of a system which is used for teaching the Spanish language to English-speaking people. By reference to the above diagram, explain how this system works. (A carp is a type of fish.)

_____

_____

_____   [3]

(c)   Two groups of students were asked to remember 26 words. They had four minutes in which to learn the words for later recall.

Group A saw the 26 words classified into groups and sub-groups as follows:

		Minerals		
	Metals		Stones	
Rare	Common	Alloys	Precious	Masonry
Platinum	Aluminium	Bronze	Sapphire	Limestone
Silver	Copper	Steel	Emerald	Granite
Gold	Lead	Brass	Diamond	Marble
	Iron		Ruby	Slate

Group B saw the same 26 words but they were arranged randomly.

The results showed that there was a difference in the average number of correctly recalled words for each group.

(i) Which group do you think, on average, recalled more words?

_____ [1]

(ii) From your knowledge of memory, explain why you would expect a difference between the two groups.

_____

_____ [2]

(d) Describe **one** study which it is claimed shows that memory is an active constructive process.

_____

_____

_____

_____ [5]

(e) Explain **two** ways in which a knowledge of theories of memory could help you to revise for an examination.

_____

_____

_____

_____

_____

_____ [6]

Chapter quiz

Answer the following questions in no longer than 10 minutes:

1   Who showed that asking particular questions affected people's memory of a traffic accident?
2   What term did Bartlett use to describe how we try to make sense of information that we receive?
3   What method did Bartlett use to investigate constructive memory?
4   Which type of amnesia involves the person being unable to store new information?
5   According to Freud, what mechanism is the source of all forgetting?
6   What term is used to describe how we remember things better if we are in the same physiological condition as when we first learned them?
7   What were Bruner's three modes of representation?
8   Which theory of memory was developed by Craik and Lockhart?
9   What often-repeated information did Bekerian and Baddeley use to study the effects of repetition on memory?
10 What is the name of the mnemonic system which involves using a well-known walk or area to remember a list?

This chapter can be divided into two major segments, as follows:

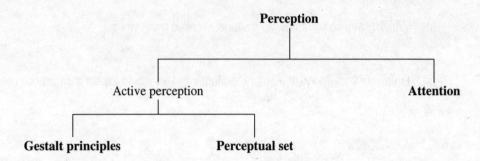

Each of those segments can then be subdivided into smaller tree diagrams. These can be useful in helping you to structure your revision.

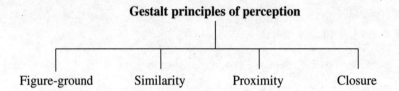

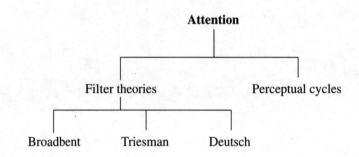

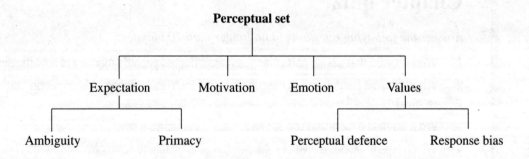

Planning an essay

When you are planning an essay for an examination, remember that you won't have enough time to write down everything you know about the subject. This means that the essay's structure is particularly important. You must bring in as much information that is relevant to the question as you can, and leave out extra or irrelevant details.

Even writing quite quickly, you will probably be able to write only one paragraph in five minutes so your essay structure must be matched to the time you have available and you should plan what the paragraphs will cover with that in mind. Using this method, a 45-minute essay involves five minutes' thinking time and produces eight paragraphs. For example:

SAMPLE
QUESTION

Describe some factors which may influence our perception.

Paragraph 1	introduction: perception and sensation
Paragraph 2	perceptual organisation: figure/ground
Paragraph 3	Gestalt laws
Paragraph 4	perceptual set: influencing factors
Paragraph 5	expectation: study and implications
Paragraph 6	motivation: study and implications
Paragraph 7	anticipatory schemas and the perceptual cycle
Paragraph 8	conclusion: perception as an active process

This isn't the only way of tackling this essay, of course. There are other possibilities which would be equally acceptable. Try producing some essay outlines for yourself, using the following questions:

QUESTIONS

1   *In what sense can human perception be considered active? Give evidence for your answer.*
2   *Discuss some of the characteristics of perceptual set.*
3   *Outline and discuss some models of selective attention.*
4   *How far can Neisser's model explain psychological findings about perceptual processes?*

Question 1:	*In what sense can human perception be considered active? Give evidence for your answer.*
Paragraph 1	introduction:
Paragraph 2	
Paragraph 3	
Paragraph 4	
Paragraph 5	
Paragraph 6	
Paragraph 7	
Paragraph 8	conclusion:

Question 2:	*Discuss some of the characteristics of perceptual set.*
Paragraph 1	introduction:
Paragraph 2	
Paragraph 3	
Paragraph 4	

Paragraph 5

Paragraph 6

Paragraph 7

Paragraph 8   conclusion:

Question 3:   *Outline and discuss some models of selective attention.*

Paragraph 1   introduction:

Paragraph 2

Paragraph 3

Paragraph 4

Paragraph 5

Paragraph 6

Paragraph 7

Paragraph 8   conclusion:

Question 4:   *How far can Neisser's model explain psychological findings about perceptual processes?*

Paragraph 1   introduction:

Paragraph 2

Paragraph 3

Paragraph 4

Paragraph 5

Paragraph 6

Paragraph 7

Paragraph 8   conclusion:

Chapter summary

(*Psychology: an Introduction*, page 217)

1   Perception is the brain actively interpreting the information which it receives through the senses.

2   The Gestalt psychologists identified some basic principles of perceptual organisation, which they called the Laws of Prägnanz. Some of these were: figure/ground organisation, similarity, proximity, and the principle of closure.

3   Perceptual set is a state of readiness to perceive certain things rather than others. Studies have shown how emotion, motivation and other factors can affect perceptual set.

4   Perceptual defence was put forward by Postman et al. to explain why we are less ready to perceive unpleasant things.

5   Work on selective attention and, in particular, the 'cocktail party problem' resulted in the development of a series of filter theories, showing how information might be filtered out.

6   Neisser's model of the perceptual cycle shows a different approach – that information which is expected or anticipated is included more strongly, rather than anything being filtered out.

Key sections for revision

1   the nature of perception
2   Laws of Prägnanz
3   perceptual set
4   perceptual defence
5   selective attention
6   Neisser's perceptual cycle

Issues and perspectives

Using the following table, note down any features of interest which relate to the key sections of the chapter.

Key section	Methods of study	Evaluation and criticism	Ethical issues
1 the nature of perception			
2 Laws of Prägnanz			
3 perceptual set			
4 perceptual defence			
5 selective attention			
6 Neisser's perceptual cycle			

Revision questions

Short-answer questions are useful for testing your knowledge of an area while you are revising, and for making sure that you understand it. They also often appear in examinations, and when they do you will have only a limited amount of time to answer them. The questions will be marked according to the information you have used to answer them and what you can attain marks for will be set out in a mark scheme.

Here are two 10-mark questions, with typical marking schemes which an examiner might use to assess answers.

Briefly describe the factors which can induce perceptual set.

perception/perceptual set	(up to)	2 marks
expectation, primacy, motivation, emotion, values (2 marks each)	(up to)	8 marks
	(minimum 4 factors for full marks)	
	Total 10 marks	

Describe Neisser's perceptual cycle, using a specific example.

elements of cycle (2 marks each)	(up to)	6 marks
appropriate example	(up to)	3 marks
continuous nature of cycle		1 mark
	Total 10 marks	

As you can see, each question has its own mark scheme and these share out the marks among the different types of knowledge needed to answer the question.

Bearing this in mind, try to work out your own mark schemes for each of the following questions. Each question is worth 10 marks. If you feel that you need more help, look at the mark schemes in the other chapters.

1   *What is meant by the phrase 'perception is an active process'? Give an example.*

2   *Describe the Gestalt principles of perception.*

3   *Describe and discuss a study which shows how either motivation or emotion can influence perception.*

4   *Outline Triesman's model of selective attention.*

5   *Describe and discuss Worthington's study of perceptual defence.*

When you have written your mark scheme, turn to the relevant pages in your textbook and make sure that your scheme reflects the information covered by that topic.

Answering revision questions

Now try answering each of these questions, giving yourself 15 minutes to complete each one. At the end of that time, mark your answer, using the mark scheme that you have developed.

(NB: It is essential that you write the mark scheme <u>before</u> you try to answer the question! Doing it the other way round would be completely pointless because you would be too influenced by what you have already written.)

QUESTIONS

1   *What is meant by the phrase 'perception is an active process'? Give an example.*

2   *Describe the Gestalt principles of perception.*

3   *Describe and discuss a study which shows how either motivation or emotion can influence perception.*

4   *Outline Triesman's model of selective attention.*

5   *Describe and discuss Worthington's study of perceptual defence.*

A suggestion for practical work

This study has been derived from Exercise 12.1 suggested on page 208 of *Psychology: an Introduction*. It is an experiment which will allow you to look at how expectation influences perception. You will need to perform the task with several people and mark the scores according to whether their answer was the same as the previous ones or different.

Carrying out the study

In planning your study, you will need to identify the following (consult Chapter 22, pages 424–8 of *Psychology: an Introduction* if you need further explanation):

hypothesis _____

null hypothesis _____

independent variable _____

dependent variable _____

controls _____

ethical considerations _____

_____

_____

_____

_____

Make notes on how you will carry out this study. _____

_____

_____

_____

_____

Analysing the results

You will need a summary table of results which includes the total correct answers given for each condition: numbers and letters. It should be called Table 1 and will need a title telling your reader exactly what it is about. Consult Appendix 2A (page 205) for help in drawing up your table.

You will also need a diagram to display your findings visually. This will be called Fig. 1 and will be a bar chart showing the total scores from the two sets of data. One of the bars will represent the 'letters' condition and the other will represent the 'numbers' condition.

Reporting the study

You are now ready to write up your experiment in the correct format.

Use Checklist A in the Appendix (page 210) to make sure you have included everything you need to.

Sample examination question

Northern Examining Association, June 1990
Paper 2, Question 1
Paper reference: 2175

1   The picture below will be perceived differently if you turn it upside down.

(a)   What is meant by the term "perception"? Use the picture above to explain your answer.

....

....

....   [3]

(b)

The various retinal images produced by opening and closing a door are quite different and yet we do not perceive a series of different doors.

location constancy.   ☐   (Tick the correct box.)

perceptual closure.   ☐

shape constancy.   ☐

motion parallax.   ☐

[2]

(c)   Two students were shown the following series of pictures.

Student A was shown the pictures, one at a time, going from 1 to 12 (girl changing to wolf).
Student B was shown the pictures one at a time, going from 12 to 1 (wolf changing to girl).

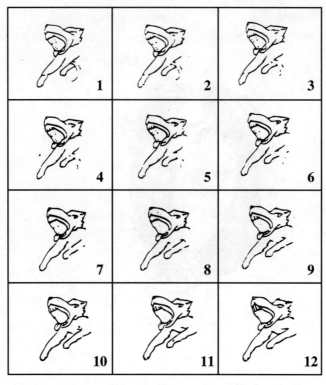

After briefly seeing each picture the students were asked what they saw before seeing the next picture. The two students differed in the numbers of pictures of wolves they reported seeing.

(i)   Which student do you think reported seeing more pictures of a wolf?

_____ [1]

(ii)   Which student do you think reported seeing more pictures of a girl?

_____ [1]

(iii) From your knowledge of perception, explain why different results were obtained from the two students.

_____

_____ [3]

(d)   Describe **one** study which investigates the way that perceptual processes can be influenced by motivation.

_____

_____

_____ [5]

(e)   Describe and explain any **two** perceptual illusions that you have come across in your everyday life.

_____

_____

_____

_____ [6]

Chapter quiz

Answer the following questions in no longer than 10 minutes:

1   Which group of psychologists discovered the principles of perception which include similarity and proximity?

2   What fundamental perceptual principle forms the basis for pattern perception and our ability to identify objects?

3   What name is given to our tendency to perceive complete objects even if the stimulus is really incomplete?

4   What factor influencing perceptual set did Gilchrist and Nesburg study?

5   What is the term used for perceiving something without being aware of it?

6   Who used split-span tests to study attention?

7   In Cherry's dichotic listening tasks, what activity made sure that participants were really attending to the correct message? (Give the correct term.)

8   Who suggested that perceptual filters might attenuate an unattended signal, rather than block it out altogether?

9   What term is used to describe processing a signal for meaning, rather than for its physical characteristics?

10   What hypothetical mental structures did Neisser identify as the basis of our cognition?

Chapter 13 – Theories of personality

This chapter can be divided into three major segments, as follows:

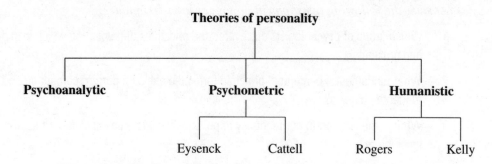

Each of those segments can then be subdivided into smaller tree diagrams. These can be useful in helping you to structure your revision.

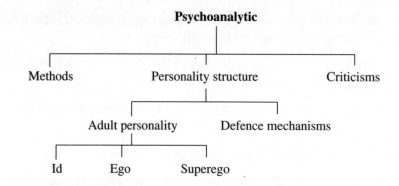

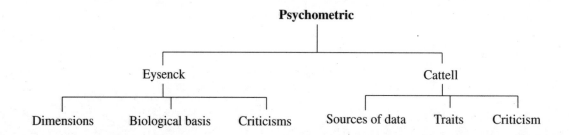

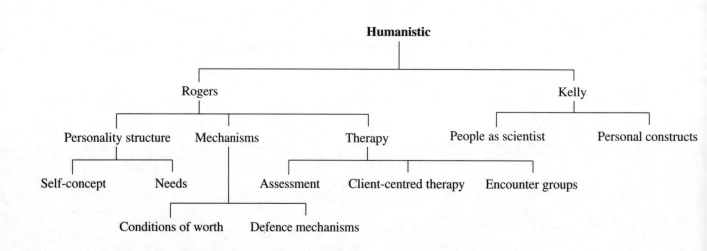

Planning an essay

When you are planning an essay for an examination, remember that you won't have enough time to write down everything you know about the subject. This means that the essay's structure is particularly important. You must bring in as much information that is relevant to the question as you can, and leave out extra or irrelevant details.

Even writing quite quickly, you will probably be able to write only one paragraph in five minutes, so your essay structure must be matched to the time you have available and you should plan what the paragraphs will cover with that in mind. Using this method, a 45-minute essay involves five minutes' thinking time and produces eight paragraphs. For example:

SAMPLE QUESTION

Outline and critically discuss Freud's theory of adult personality.

Paragraph 1	introduction: Freud as major figure of his time
Paragraph 2	methods: free-association, dream analysis, etc.
Paragraph 3	structure of adult personality: id, ego superego
Paragraph 4	conflicts between aspects of personality
Paragraph 5	defence mechanisms
Paragraph 6	criticisms of methods and 'psychological truth'
Paragraph 7	criticisms of psychoanalysis as therapy
Paragraph 8	conclusion: some use, but limited validity for modern times

Of course, this isn't the only way you could tackle this essay and you wouldn't have to come to the same conclusions either. However, you would have to demonstrate your knowledge of the theory and its criticisms. Try producing some essay outlines for yourself, using the following questions:

QUESTIONS

1   *Distinguish between idiographic and nomothetic theories of personality. Give examples.*
2   *What are the strengths and weaknesses of the trait approach to personality?*
3   *How are humanistic theories of personality different from trait approaches? Give reasons for your answer.*
4   *Outline and critically discuss personal construct theory.*

Question 1:	*Distinguish between idiographic and nomothetic theories of personality. Give examples.*
Paragraph 1	introduction:
Paragraph 2	
Paragraph 3	
Paragraph 4	
Paragraph 5	
Paragraph 6	
Paragraph 7	
Paragraph 8	conclusion:

Question 2:	*What are the strengths and weaknesses of the trait approach to personality?*
Paragraph 1	introduction:
Paragraph 2	

Paragraph 3

Paragraph 4

Paragraph 5

Paragraph 6

Paragraph 7

Paragraph 8   conclusion:

Question 3:   *How are humanistic theories of personality different from trait approaches? Give reasons for your answer.*

Paragraph 1   introduction:

Paragraph 2

Paragraph 3

Paragraph 4

Paragraph 5

Paragraph 6

Paragraph 7

Paragraph 8   conclusion:

Question 4:   *Outline and critically discuss personal construct theory.*

Paragraph 1   introduction:

Paragraph 2

Paragraph 3

Paragraph 4

Paragraph 5

Paragraph 6

Paragraph 7

Paragraph 8   conclusion:

Chapter summary

(*Psychology: an Introduction*, page 245)

1   Personality theories may be divided into two main kinds: idiographic theories, which study the individual in depth, and nomothetic theories, which look for characteristics which people have in common.

2   Freud considered that personality consisted of three parts: id, ego and superego. A dynamic balance among them was maintained by the ego.

3   The ego develops defence mechanisms which protect it from threat, which can mean that hidden traumas affect the person without their knowledge.

4   H. J. Eysenck developed a 'trait' theory of personality, in which he identified two major traits: extraversion and neuroticism. He suggested that these arose from underlying inherited biological factors.

5   Cattell's theory of personality suggested that there were 16 major personality traits which affected the individual's behaviour.

6   Carl Rogers put forward a humanistic theory of personality, suggesting that we have two basic needs: the need for positive regard and the need for self-actualisation. Each of these needs must be expressed or the individual will develop problems.

7   Kelly developed a theory of personal constructs, which explained how the individual makes sense of the world.

Key sections for revision

1 idiographic and nomothetic approaches
2 Freudian theory
3 ego-defence mechanisms
4 Eysenck's trait theory
5 Cattell's trait theory
6 Rogers's humanistic theory
7 personal construct theory

Issues and perspectives

Using the following table, note down any features of interest which relate to the key sections of the chapter.

Key section	Methods of study	Evaluation and criticism	Etihcal issues
1 idiographic and nomothetic approaches			
2 Freudian theory			
3 ego-defence mechanisms			
4 Eysenck's trait theory			
5 Cattell's trait theory			
6 Rogers's humanistic theory			
7 personal construct theory			

Revision questions

Short-answer questions are useful for testing your knowledge of an area while you are revising, and for making sure that you understand it. They also often appear in examinations, and when they do you will have only a limited amount of time to answer them. The questions will be marked according to the information you have used to answer them and what you can attain marks for will be set out in a mark scheme.

Here are two 10-mark questions, with typical marking schemes which an examiner might use to assess answers.

Briefly describe Freud's model of personality.

'iceberg' model of mind		1 mark
id	(up to)	2 marks
ego	(up to)	2 marks
superego	(up to)	2 marks
dynamic balance/threat,etc.	(up to)	3 marks
		Total 10 marks

How did Eysenck suggest that biological factors produced extraversion and neuroticism?

description of extraversion	(up to)	2 marks
description of neuroticism	(up to)	2 marks
neural inhibition/excitation, etc. (3 marks only if explicitly related to extraversion)	(up to)	3 marks
autonomic arousal etc. (3 marks only if explicitly related to neuroticism)	(up to)	3 marks
		Total 10 marks

As you can see, each question has its own mark scheme and these share out the marks between the different types of knowledge needed to answer the question.

Bearing this in mind, try to work out your own mark schemes for each of the following questions. Each question is worth 10 marks.

1   *Distinguish between idiographic and nomothetic theories of personality. Give examples.*

2   *What are defence mechanisms? Give four different examples of defence mechanisms.*

3   *What three sources of data did Cattell use to develop his theory of personality?*

4   *Discuss the relationship between the need for positive regard and the need for self-actualisation.*

5   *What are personal constructs and how can they be investigated?*

When you have written your mark scheme, turn to the relevant pages in your textbook and make sure that your scheme reflects the information covered by that topic.

Answering revision questions

Now try answering each of these questions, giving yourself 15 minutes to complete each one. At the end of that time, mark your answer, using the mark scheme that you have developed.

(NB: It is essential that you write the mark scheme before you try to answer the question! Doing it the other way round would be completely pointless because you would be too influenced by what you have already written.)

1   *Distinguish between idiographic and nomothetic theories of personality. Give examples.*

2   *What are defence mechanisms? Give <u>four</u> different examples of defence mechanisms.*

3   *What <u>three</u> sources of data did Cattell use to develop his theory of personality?*

4   *Discuss the relationship between the need for positive regard and the need for self-actualisation.*

5   *What are personal constructs and how can they be investigated?*

A suggestion for practical work

This study has been derived from Exercise 13.1, suggested on page 235 of *Psychology: an Introduction*. It is a correlation study which will allow you to see whether a measure of brain activity like the Necker cube correlates with scores on Eysenck's personality test.

You will need to carry out your test on several people in order to get enough scores to correlate.

Carrying out the study

In planning your study, you will need to identify the following (consult Chapter 22, pages 424–8 of *Psychology: an Introduction* if you need further explanation):

hypothesis _____

null hypothesis _____

variable 1 _____

variable 2 _____

controls _____

ethical considerations _____

Make notes on how you will carry out this study. _____

Analysing the results

You will need to draw up a scattergram to show the relationship between your two variables. Use the notes in Appendix 2D (page 208) to help you to do this.

Reporting the study

You are now ready to write up your experiment in the correct format.

Use Checklist B in the Appendix (page 210) to make sure you have included everything you need to.

Sample examination questions

Midlands Examining Group, February 1990
Individual Differences Module, Source A, Questions 1/5
Paper reference: 723

The Trait Approach to Personality

One way that psychologists have tried to study personality is by identifying the basic traits or characteristics which make up an individual's personality. If you describe people as being intelligent, or aggressive, you are using trait terms to describe them. Cattell has identified 16 basic personality traits and has devised a questionnaire to measure them. The questionnaire is called the 16PF and consists of questions to which the subject answers yes or no. The diagram below shows the personality profiles for two groups of people, scientists and artists.

A. reserved

B. less intelligent

C. affected by feelings

E. submissive

F. serious

G. expedient

H. timid

I. tough minded

L. trusting

M. practical

N. forthright

O. self assured

Q_1 conservative

Q_2 group dependent

Q_3 uncontrolled

Q_4 relaxed

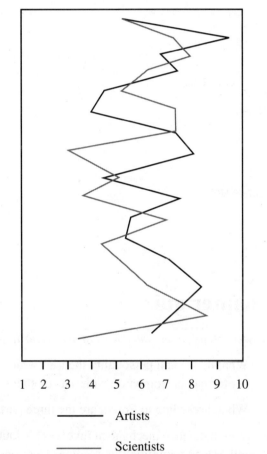

outgoing

more intelligent

emotionally stable

dominant

happy-go-lucky

conscientious

venturesome

sensitive

imaginative

shrewd

apprehensive

experimenting

self sufficient

controlled

tense

——— Artists

——— Scientists

1   How many traits does Cattell identify in his questionnaire?

_____ [1]

2   What is the *trait approach* to personality?

_____ [1]

3   The 16PF questionnaire involves the subject answering yes/no to the questions. What are **two** problems with measuring personality in this way?

Problem 1

Problem 2

_____

_____

_____ [4]

4   List **two** traits on which artists and scientists are similar, according to the personality profiles.

_____

_____ [2]

5   One criticism of Cattell's theory is that it doesn't explain how personality traits develop. Other theories are more flexible and describe personality development. Choose one of the following theories and say how it is different from Catell's theory of personality.

Eysenck's theory   ☐

Rogers' theory   ☐

Kelly's theory   ☐

Difference 1

_____

_____

Difference 2

_____

_____ [4]

Chapter quiz

Answer the following questions in no longer than 10 minutes:

1   What do we call personality theories which aim to produce general results so that people can be compared with one another?

2   What, according to Freud, are the three parts of the adult personality?

3   Which defence mechanism involves attributing a 'bad' thought to another person, rather than admitting that it comes from oneself?

4   What name did Freud give to the general life-energy which he saw as the basis of motivation?

5   Apart from extraversion, what was the other main dimension of personality in Eysenck's theory?

6   What biological structure did Eysenck claim was responsible for extraversion?

7   Cattell used L-data, Q-data and T-data in formulating his theory. What does the 'L' stand for?

8   Rogers identified two basic needs of human beings. One was the need for positive regard, what was the other?

9   What method did Rogers develop for measuring the effectiveness of therapy?

10 What, according to Kelly, are the mental structures that we use to make sense of the world?

Chapter 14 – Psychometrics

This chapter can be divided into three major segments, as follows:

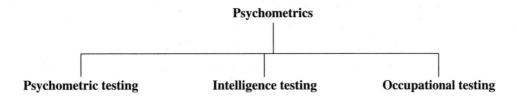

Each of those segments can then be subdivided into smaller tree diagrams. These can be useful in helping you to structure your revision.

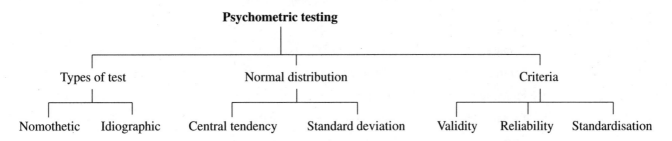

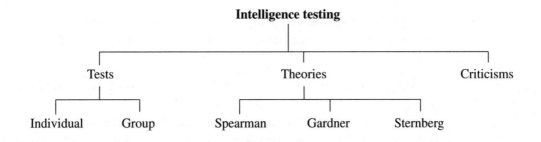

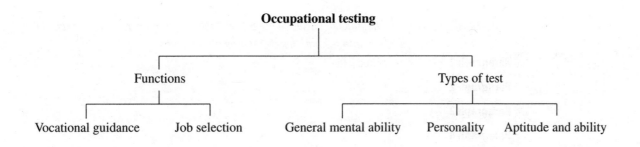

Planning an essay

When you are planning an essay for an examination, remember that you won't have enough time to write down everything you know about the subject. This means that the essay's structure is particularly important. You must bring in as much information that is relevant to the question as you can, and leave out extra or irrelevant details.

Even writing quite quickly, you will probably be able to write only one paragraph in five minutes, so your essay structure must be matched to the time you have available and you should plan what the paragraphs will cover with that in mind. Using this method, a 45-minute essay involves five minutes' thinking time and produces eight paragraphs. For example:

Sample Question

Describe and discuss the process of intelligence testing.

Paragraph 1	introduction: origins: Binet's first test
Paragraph 2	age-related IQ and individual testing
Paragraph 3	group-based testing
Paragraph 4	the concept of 'g'
Paragraph 5	Guildford's theory of intelligence
Paragraph 6	IQ tests as reflecting theoretical beliefs
Paragraph 7	problems with IQ tests
Paragraph 8	conclusion: Sternberg's three aspects of intelligence: testing only measures one

This isn't the only possible way of answering this question, of course. There are many other ways. Try producing some essay outlines for yourself, using the following questions:

Questions

1   *Distinguish between nomothetic and idiographic tests and discuss the advantages and disadvantages of each type.*
2   *Discuss issues of reliability, validity and standardisation in test construction.*
3   *Giving examples, discuss how different theories of intelligence can produce different types of test.*
4   *Describe the main types of occupational tests and how they are used.*

Question 1:	*Distinguish between nomothetic and idiographic tests and discuss the advantages and disadvantages of each type.*
Paragraph 1	introduction:
Paragraph 2	
Paragraph 3	
Paragraph 4	
Paragraph 5	
Paragraph 6	
Paragraph 7	
Paragraph 8	conclusion:

Question 2:	*Discuss issues of reliability, validity and standardisation in test construction.*
Paragraph 1	introduction:
Paragraph 2	
Paragraph 3	
Paragraph 4	

Paragraph 5

Paragraph 6

Paragraph 7

Paragraph 8   conclusion:

Question 3:   *Giving examples,discuss how different theories of intelligence can produce different types of test.*

Paragraph 1   introduction:

Paragraph 2

Paragraph 3

Paragraph 4

Paragraph 5

Paragraph 6

Paragraph 7

Paragraph 8   conclusion:

Question 4:   *Describe the main types of occupational tests and how they are used.*

Paragraph 1   introduction:

Paragraph 2

Paragraph 3

Paragraph 4

Paragraph 5

Paragraph 6

Paragraph 7

Paragraph 8   conclusion:

Chapter summary

(*Psychology: an Introduction*, page 266)

1   Nomothetic tests attempt to generalise about populations, whereas idiographic tests attempt to present a detailed picture of one individual.

2   Nomothetic psychometric tests are based around the idea of the normal distribution curve which has mathematical properties enabling us to say how typical a single score is of the population as a whole.

3   All reputable psychometric tests need to go through rigorous validity, reliability and standardisation procedures.

4   Early tests of intelligence used age to establish IQ scores, whereas later tests used the norms for that person's group instead. Some intelligence tests have to be individually administered; others can be applied to large groups.

5   There has been much debate as to whether there is a general 'g' factor in intelligence, or whether it is a collection of diverse skills. The triarchic model presents intelligence as a combination of context, experience and mental skills.

6   Occupational tests are used for vocational guidance, job selection and in choosing people for promotion. Feedback to the candidate, as well as to the employer, is important.

7   Occupational tests can be divided into three kinds: general mental ability tests, personality tests, and tests of job aptitude and ability. People administering these tests must be specially trained.

Key sections for revision

1   nomothetic and idiographic tests
2   the normal distribution curve
3   validity, reliability and standardisation
4   intelligence testing
5   models of intelligence
6   uses of occupational tests
7   types of occupational test

Issues and perspectives

Using the following table, note down any features of interest which relate to the key sections of the chapter.

Key section	Methods of study	Evaluation and criticism	Ethical issues
1 nomothetic and idiographic tests			
2 the normal distribution curve			
3 validity, reliability and standardisation			
4 intelligence testing			
5 models of intelligence			
6 uses of occupational tests			
7 types of occupational test			

Revision questions

Short-answer questions are useful for testing your knowledge of an area while you are revising, and for making sure that you understand it. They also often appear in examinations, and when they do you will have only a limited amount of time to answer them. The questions will be marked according to the information you have used to answer them and what you can attain marks for will be set out in a mark scheme.

Here are two 10-mark questions, with typical marking schemes which an examiner might use to assess answers.

Compare and contrast a named individual IQ test with a named group IQ test.

names of appropriate tests	(up to)	2 marks
descriptions of tests	(up to)	2 marks
differences between tests	(up to)	3 marks
similarities between tests	(up to)	3 marks
		Total 10 mark

Describe the three main types of occupational test.

definition of occupational tests		1 mark
general mental ability tests	(up to)	3 marks
personality tests	(up to)	3 marks
aptitude/ability tests	(up to)	3 marks
		Total 10 marks

As you can see, each question has its own mark scheme and these share out the marks between the different types of knowledge needed to answer the question.

Bearing this in mind, try to work out your own mark schemes for each of the following questions. Each question is worth 10 marks. If you feel that you need more help, look at the mark schemes in the other chapters.

1   *Give an example of one nomothetic and one idiographic personality test.*

2   *Briefly describe the normal distribution curve and outline its importance for psychometric testing.*

3   *Discuss the use of validity, reliability and standardisation in test development.*

4   *Explain the triarchic theory of intelligence, using a specific example to illustrate your answer.*

5   *What are the main uses of occupational tests?*

When you have written your mark scheme, turn to the relevant pages in your textbook and make sure that your scheme reflects the information covered by that topic.

Answering revision questions

Now try answering each of these questions, giving yourself 15 minutes to complete each one. At the end of that time, mark your answer, using the mark scheme that you have developed.

(NB: It is essential that you write the mark scheme before you try to answer the question! Doing it the other way round would be completely pointless because you would be too influenced by what you have already written.)

 **QUESTIONS**

1   Give an example of <u>one</u> nomothetic and <u>one</u> idiographic personality test.

2   Briefly describe the normal distribution curve and outline its importance for psychometric testing.

3   Discuss the use of validity, reliability and standardisation in test development.

4   Explain the triarchic theory of intelligence, using a specific example to illustrate your answer.

5   What are the main uses of occupational tests?

A suggestion for practical work

This study has been derived from Exercise 14.2 suggested on page 265 of *Psychology: an Introduction*. It is an exercise in developing a psychometric test for the 'job' of student, using work-sampling techniques.

You will need to begin by developing a set of work-samples, representing different aspects of a student's 'job', and you will need to try them out on several people.

Carrying out the study

In planning your study, you will need to consider the following (consult Chapter 14, pages 246–51, and Chapter 22, pages 424–8 of *Psychology: an Introduction* if you need further explanation):

target population _____

test elements _____

test design and organisation _____

controls and precautions _____

sampling procedures _____

Ethical considerations _____

_____

_____

_____

_____

_____

Make notes on how you will carry out this study. _____

_____

_____

_____

_____

Analysing the results

You will need to summarise the results obtained when you pilot the test. Draw a bar chart to display the results from your pilot sample visually. Consult Appendix 2B (page 205) for help in drawing this up. This should be called Fig. 1 and will need an appropriate title.

Reliability tests can be illustrated using a scattergram. Consult Appendix 2D (page 208) for help in drawing this up. This should be called Fig. 2, and will need an appropriate title.

Reporting the study

You are now ready to write up your experiment in the correct format.

Use Checklist D in the Appendix (page 211) to make sure you have included everything you need to.

Sample examination question

Midlands Examining Group, June 1990
Individual Differences Module, Source A, Questions 1/4
Paper reference: 757

NEW FROM SCOOBY ENTERPRISES
(The Company that Measures the Mind)

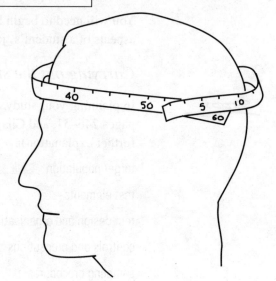

THE PSYCHOMEASURE INTELLIGENCE TEST
For only £25.00 (plus P&P) you can have the
equipment to measure the intelligence of your
friends, employees, teachers etc.

Easy to use and quick to analyse the
PSYCHOMEASURE offers the ideal alternative
to time consuming I.Q. tests. All you have to do
is to place the PSYCHOMEASURE around the
forehead of the subject and read off the
intelligence score.

Validity refers to whether a test measures the
quality that it sets out to measure.

Reliability refers to whether the test gives a consistent measure of someone's performance.

QUESTIONS

1   Which of the following statements best describes the PSYCHOMEASURE INTELLIGENCE
     TEST? Put a tick against your answer.

(a)   The test is reliable and valid   ☐

(b)   The test is reliable but not valid   ☐

(c)   The test is valid but not reliable   ☐

(d)   The test is neither reliable nor valid   ☐   [1]

2   Describe **ONE** way that you could assess the reliability of the PSYCHOMEASURE test.

_____

_____

_____

_____   [2]

3   Describe **ONE** way that you could assess the validity of the PSYCHOMEASURE test.

_____

_____

_____

_____   [2]

4   Most I.Q. tests have a bias in them that gives certain people better scores than others.
     Describe **one** bias in the PSYCHOMEASURE INTELLIGENCE TEST.

_____

_____

_____   [2]

Chapter quiz

Answer the following questions in no longer than 10 minutes:

1   What do we call tests which are concerned with looking at a single person's distinctive characteristics?

2   What mathematical construct forms the basis of nomothetic testing?

3   Reliability and validity are two of the three fundamentals of test design. What is the third?

4   Who developed the formula for calculating IQ based on mental age?

5   If an IQ based on mental age is age-related IQ, what is an IQ based on the average score for the person's group?

6   What does 'g' stand for in intelligence testing?

7   How many types of intelligence did Gardner identify?

8   What are the three aspects of intelligence identified by Sternberg?

9   There are three main types of occupational test. General mental ability tests and personality tests are two of them. What is the third?

10   What type of test is used to see whether someone has the mental abilities and inclinations that they may need for a new job?

This chapter can be divided into three major segments, as follows:

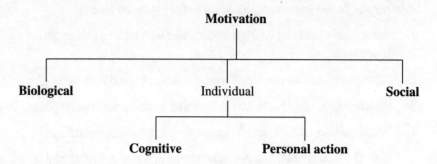

Each of those segments can then be subdivided into smaller tree diagrams. These can be useful in helping you to structure your revision.

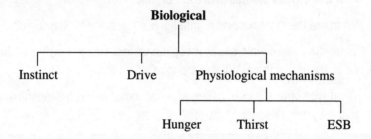

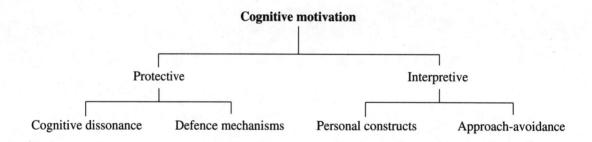

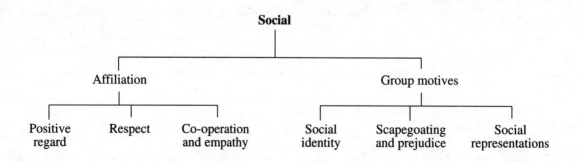

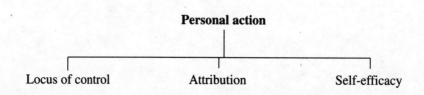

Planning an essay

When you are planning an essay for an examination, remember that you won't have enough time to write down everything you know about the subject. This means that the essay's structure is particularly important. You must bring in as much information that is relevant to the question as you can, and leave out extra or irrelevant details.

Even writing quite quickly, you will probably be able to write only one paragraph in five minutes, so your essay structure must be matched to the time you have available and you should plan what the paragraphs will cover with that in mind. Using this method, a 45-minute essay involves five minutes' thinking time and produces eight paragraphs. For example:

Outline and discuss some of the major mechanisms of human motivation.

Paragraph 1	introduction: motivation as energising behaviour
Paragraph 2	instinct and drive theories
Paragraph 3	physiological motives: hunger and obesity
Paragraph 4	cognitive dissonance
Paragraph 5	defence mechanisms
Paragraph 6	locus of control and self-efficacy
Paragraph 7	affiliation and social motives
Paragraph 8	conclusion: many levels of human motivation, all influential

This isn't the only way of tackling this question, of course. Try producing some essay outlines for yourself, using the following questions:

1   *How may knowledge of physiological mechanisms of motivation help us to understand human behaviour?*
2   *How does human motivation differ from that of animals?*
3   *How may attributions and self-efficacy beliefs influence human motivation?*
4   *'Human motivation is essentially a social process.' Do you agree? Give reasons for your answer.*

Question 1:	*How may knowledge of physiological mechanisms of motivation help us to understand human behaviour?*
Paragraph 1	introduction:
Paragraph 2	
Paragraph 3	
Paragraph 4	
Paragraph 5	
Paragraph 6	
Paragraph 7	
Paragraph 8	conclusion:

Question 2:	*How does human motivation differ from that of animals?*
Paragraph 1	introduction:
Paragraph 2	
Paragraph 3	
Paragraph 4	
Paragraph 5	
Paragraph 6	

Paragraph 7

Paragraph 8   conclusion:

Question 3:   *How may attributions and self-efficacy beliefs influence human motivation?*

Paragraph 1   introduction:

Paragraph 2

Paragraph 3

Paragraph 4

Paragraph 5

Paragraph 6

Paragraph 7

Paragraph 8   conclusion:

Question 4:   *'Human motivation is essentially a social process.' Do you agree? Give reasons for your answer.*

Paragraph 1   introduction:

Paragraph 2

Paragraph 3

Paragraph 4

Paragraph 5

Paragraph 6

Paragraph 7

Paragraph 8   conclusion:

Chapter summary

(*Psychology: an Introduction*, page 285)

1   Early psychological theories of motivation argued that motivation came from 'instincts' – inherited forces that compelled certain kinds of behaviour.

2   Drive theories of motivation assume that an organism (person or animal) is trying to maintain homeostasis, and that motivated behaviour aims to restore homeostatic balance.

3   Physiological sources of motivation have shown that brain mechanisms are strongly involved in motivational states like hunger and thirst. Electrical stimulation of the brain is also a strong motivator.

4   Cognitive mechanisms of motivation include the processes of cognitive dissonance, defence mechanisms, personal constructs and cognitive interpretations of approach-avoidance conflicts.

5   Motivating personal action involves psychological mechanisms such as locus of control, self-efficacy beliefs and attribution styles. Learned helplessness is a state where motivation to take personal action is seriously depleted, as previous experience has suggested that it is not worth trying.

6   People have powerful affiliation motives which motivate them to get on with others. These include a personal need for positive regard, a social need for respect, the tendency to co-operate rather than to confront and empathy.

7   Social and group motives include the way that people identify with in-groups through social identification, how prejudice can increase through scapegoating and how shared social representations influence how people are motivated to undertake social action.

Key sections for revision

1 instinct theories
2 drive theories
3 physiological motivation
4 cognitive motivation
5 control and efficacy
6 affiliation
7 social and group motivation

Issues and perspectives

Using the following table, note down any features of interest which relate to the key sections of the chapter.

Key section	Methods of study	Evaluation and criticism	Ethical issues
1 instinct theories			
2 drive theories			
3 physiological motivation			
4 cognitive motivation			
5 control and efficacy			
6 affiliation			
7 social and group motivation			

Revision questions

Short-answer questions are useful for testing your knowledge of an area while you are revising, and for making sure that you understand it. They also often appear in examinations, and when they do you will have only a limited amount of time to answer them. The questions will be marked according to the information you have used to answer them and what you can attain marks for will be set out in a mark scheme.

Here are two 10-mark questions, with typical marking schemes which an examiner might use to assess answers.

Describe and discuss Olds and Milner's study of electrical stimulation of the brain.

description of study	(up to)	4 marks
outcome of study	(up to)	3 marks
implications/discussion	(up to)	3 marks
		Total 10 marks

Outline three affiliative mechanisms of motivation.

definition of motivation		1 mark
social respect	(up to)	3 marks
empathy	(up to)	3 marks
co-operation/reconciliation (aggression acceptable if explanation/justification provided)	(up to)	3 marks
		Total 10 marks

As you can see, each question has its own mark scheme and these share out the marks between the different types of knowledge needed to answer the question.

Bearing this in mind, try to work out your own mark schemes for each of the following questions. Each question is worth 10 marks. If you feel that you need more help, look at the mark schemes in the other chapters.

1   *What problems arise from the use of 'instincts' to explain motivation?*

2   *What is the drive theory approach to motivation? Give an example.*

3   *Describe and discuss a study of cognitive dissonance.*

4   *Discuss the relationship between the concepts of locus of control, self-efficacy and learned helplessness.*

5   *What are social representations? Give <u>one</u> example of a social representation which has been studied by psychologists.*

When you have written your mark scheme, turn to the relevant pages in your textbook and make sure that your scheme reflects the information covered by that topic.

Answering revision questions

Now try answering each of these questions, giving yourself 15 minutes to complete each one. At the end of that time, mark your answer, using the mark scheme that you have developed.

(NB: It is essential that you write the mark scheme <u>before</u> you try to answer the question! Doing it the other way round would be completely pointless because you would be too influenced by what you have already written.)

QUESTIONS   1   *What problems arise from the use of 'instincts' to explain motivation?*

2   *What is the drive theory approach to motivation? Give an example.*

3   *Describe and discuss a study of cognitive dissonance.*

4   *Discuss the relationship between the concepts of locus of control, self-efficacy and learned helplessness.*

5   *What are social representations? Give <u>one</u> example of a social representation which has been studied by psychologists.*

A suggestion for practical work

This study has been derived from Exercise 15.2 suggested on page 271 of *Psychology: an Introduction*. It is an experiment which will allow you to investigate the effect that motivation can have on perception.

You will need to ask several people in order to obtain enough scores for comparison.

Carrying out the study

In planning your study, you will need to identify the following (consult Chapter 22, pages 424–8 of *Psychology: an Introduction* if you need further explanation):

hypothesis _____

null hypothesis _____

independent variable _____

dependent variable _____

controls _____

design _____

ethical considerations _____

_____

_____

_____

_____

_____

Make notes on how you will carry out this study. _____

_____

_____

_____

_____

Analysing the results

You will need a summary table of results which includes the mean, median and mode for your two groups. It should be called Table 1 and will need a title telling your reader exactly what it is about. Consult Appendix 2A (page 205) if you need help with this.

You will also need a diagram to display your findings visually. This will be called Fig. 1 and should be a bar chart showing the mean scores for the before-lunch and after-lunch conditions. Use the notes in Appendix 2B (page 205) to draw up a bar chart of your findings.

Reporting the study

You are now ready to write up your experiment in the correct format.

Use Checklist A in the Appendix (page 210) to make sure you have included everything you need to.

Sample examination questions

> Midlands Examining Group, Specimen paper 1987
> Comparative Module, Source B, Questions 4/7

"Did you see that thing about those football hooligans yesterday?" Fatima asked. "It was really nasty – they were beating people up and I hear that some people even got stabbed. One of them's in hospital now. Just like animals, they are!"

"Yeah," said Reg. "I read somewhere that it really is being like an animal. This biologist reckoned that it was all a result of an instinct that we've got, and that we have to be able to let our aggression out. He said that we all need to go in for sports and competitions and stuff, so that we can get rid of our aggressive instincts, and that's why these football hooligans are like they are."

"I think that's rubbish," Ron put in. "Anyone can see that that sort of aggression doesn't come naturally. How come we all don't do it, if it's an instinct? No, I reckon that it's all to do with frustration: I read a psychologist who was saying that it all comes from people having really stressful home lives, and high unemployment and all that. They turn aggressive because they can't do anything positive with their lives."

"Well I blame the parents myself," said Fatima. "If they'd been trained properly from when they were younger, they wouldn't be turning to violence now. When you see these children being slapped around by their parents, it's no wonder that they copy them and turn to violence later on, is it?"

"I don't know," Sharon chipped in. "I knew this guy once who said that it just wasn't like that at all. He said when you were going along to a match, as part of a gang, you really felt as if you were somebody – not just drifting along like most people do. And the violence was just a part of what you did – nothing special really."

"Well it still doesn't excuse it," said Reg.

4   What does Fatima consider to be the most important factor in the development of football hooliganism? What psychological theory is she expressing in this discussion?

factor _____ [1]

theory _____ [2]

5   What psychological theory is Reg expressing when he talks about "instincts"? What does he see as the answer to the problem of football hooliganism?

theory _____ [2]

answer _____ [1]

6   What name is given to the psychological theory that Ron is putting forward? What would he see as an answer to the problem of football hooliganism?

name _____ [1]

answer _____ [2]

7   Why does Sharon think being in a gang is important? How does this relate to the psychology that you have studied?

importance of gang _____

_____ [1]

relate to psychology _____

_____ [2]

Chapter quiz

Answer the following questions in no longer than 10 minutes:

1   What physiological concept is the basis for drive theories of motivation?

2   Which part of the brain seems to mediate satiation?

3   What animals did Grossman use to investigate neurotransmitters and motivation?

4   Who provided obese people with shelled or unshelled peanuts?

5   What does ESB stand for?

6   What cognitive motivation did Festinger et al. study in an end-of-the-world cult?

7   What is the name for the cognitive conflict resulting from a goal which has both attractive and negative components?

8   What do we call the idea that what happens to us is largely a result of our own efforts?

9   What do we call the shared ideological beliefs held by groups of people in society?

10 What under-researched social motive did Rom Harré identify?

Chapter 16 – Interpersonal perception

This chapter can be divided into four major segments, as follows:

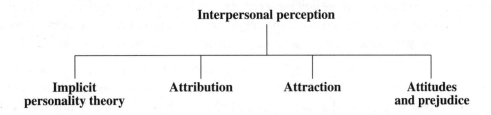

Each of those segments can then be subdivided into smaller tree diagrams. These can be useful in helping you to structure your revision.

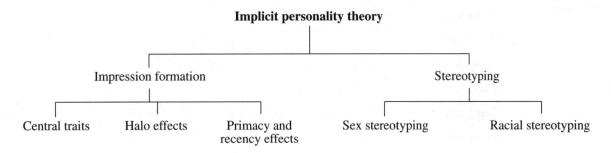

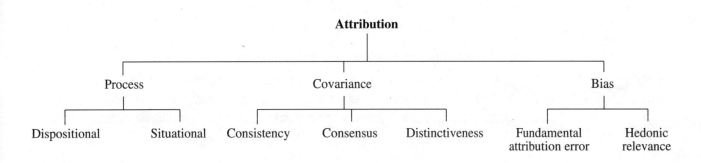

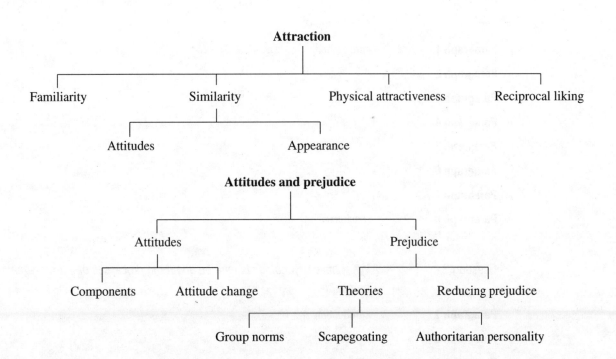

Planning an essay

When you are planning an essay for an examination, remember that you won't have enough time to write down everything you know about the subject. This means that the essay's structure is particularly important. You must bring in as much information that is relevant to the question as you can, and leave out extra or irrelevant details.

Even writing quite quickly, you will probably be able to write only one paragraph in five minutes, so your essay structure must be matched to the time you have available and you should plan what the paragraphs will cover with that in mind. Using this method, a 45-minute essay involves five minutes' thinking time and produces eight paragraphs. For example:

SAMPLE QUESTION

Why do we feel attracted to some people and not others?

Paragraph 1	introduction: attraction in social life
Paragraph 2	familiarity: Zajonc's studies
Paragraph 3	similarity of attitudes: accommodation study
Paragraph 4	Schachter's study
Paragraph 5	physical attractiveness: computer-dance study
Paragraph 6	reciprocal liking
Paragraph 7	problems of studying attraction
Paragraph 8	conclusion: studies may not resemble longer-term attraction in real life

Try producing some essay outlines for yourself, using the following questions:

QUESTIONS

1 *Outline and discuss some of the factors involved in forming impressions of other people.*
2 *What have psychologists learned about the processes of interpersonal perception?*
3 *Describe and evaluate psychological approaches to attitudes and attitude change.*
4 *How can applying psychological knowledge help us to reduce prejudice?*

Question 1:	*Outline and discuss some of the factors involved in forming impressions of other people.*
Paragraph 1	introduction:
Paragraph 2	
Paragraph 3	
Paragraph 4	
Paragraph 5	
Paragraph 6	
Paragraph 7	
Paragraph 8	conclusion:

Question 2:	*What have psychologists learned about the processes of interpersonal perception?*
Paragraph 1	introduction:
Paragraph 2	
Paragraph 3	
Paragraph 4	

Paragraph 5

Paragraph 6

Paragraph 7

Paragraph 8   conclusion:

Question 3:   *Describe and evaluate psychological approaches to attitudes and attitude change.*

Paragraph 1   introduction:

Paragraph 2

Paragraph 3

Paragraph 4

Paragraph 5

Paragraph 6

Paragraph 7

Paragraph 8   conclusion:

Question 4:   *How can applying psychological knowledge help us to reduce prejudice?*

Paragraph 1   introduction:

Paragraph 2

Paragraph 3

Paragraph 4

Paragraph 5

Paragraph 6

Paragraph 7

Paragraph 8   conclusion:

Chapter summary

(*Psychology: an Introduction*, page 312)

1   Implicit personality theories are used to form judgements about other people. These involve the grouping together of several characteristics.

2   Implicit personality theories may also lead to the stereotyping of groups of people on the basis of just one or two attributes.

3   Attribution is the process by which we provide reasons for other people's behaviour by ascribing particular causes to them. This can involve error or bias.

4   Some of the main factors in liking and attraction are familiarity, similarity, physical attraction and reciprocal liking.

5   Any attitude has three components, which can vary in strength: a cognitive part, an affective part and a behavioural part.

6   Cognitive dissonance occurs when two or more attitudes that we hold contradict each other. We tend to adjust our attitudes to remove the dissonance.

7   Prejudices are set pre-judgements of particular people or situations. They can be reduced by high social contact and by co-operation.

Key sections for revision

1 implicit personality theory
2 stereotyping
3 attribution
4 interpersonal attraction
5 attitudes
6 cognitive dissonance
7 prejudice

Issues and perspectives

Using the following table, note down any features of interest which relate to the key sections of the chapter.

Key section	Methods of study	Evaluation and criticism	Ethical issues
1 implicit personality theory			
2 stereotyping			
3 attribution			
4 interpersonal attraction			
5 attitudes			
6 cognitive dissonance			
7 prejudice			

Revision questions

Short-answer questions are useful for testing your knowledge of an area while you are revising, and for making sure that you understand it. They also often appear in examinations, and when they do you will have only a limited amount of time to answer them. The questions will be marked according to the information you have used to answer them and what you can attain marks for will be set out in a mark scheme.

Here are two 10-mark questions, with typical marking schemes which an examiner might use to assess answers.

Describe a study of implicit personality theory.

description of study	(up to)	3 marks
outcome of study	(up to)	3 marks
implications/discussion	(up to)	4 marks
		Total 10 marks

Giving a specific example, describe Kelley's theory of covariance.

process of attribution	(up to)	2 marks
use of covariance	(up to)	2 marks
consensus	(up to)	2 marks
consistency	(up to)	2 marks
distinctiveness	(up to)	2 marks
		Total 10 marks

As you can see, each question has its own mark scheme and these share out the marks between the different types of knowledge needed to answer the question.

Bearing this in mind, try to work out your own mark schemes for each of the following questions. Each question is worth 10 marks. If you feel that you need more help, look at the mark schemes in the other chapters.

1   *What is stereotyping and how can it affect our impressions of other people?*

2   *What are the main factors in attraction?*

3   *Outline the components of an attitude. Illustrate your answer with an example.*

4   *How can cognitive dissonance produce changes in attitudes?*

5   *Discuss <u>two</u> ways that prejudice can be reduced and explain why they are likely to be effective.*

When you have written your mark scheme, turn to the relevant pages in your textbook and make sure that your scheme reflects the information covered by that topic.

Answering revision questions

Now try answering each of these questions, giving yourself 15 minutes to complete each one. At the end of that time, mark your answer, using the mark scheme that you have developed.

(NB: It is essential that you write the mark scheme <u>before</u> you try to answer the question! Doing it the other way round would be completely pointless because you would be too influenced by what you have already written.)

148

1 What is stereotyping and how can it affect our impressions of other people?

2 What are the main factors in attraction?

3 Outline the components of an attitude. Illustrate your answer with an example.

4 How can cognitive dissonance produce changes in attitudes?

5 Discuss *two* ways that prejudice can be reduced, and explain why they are likely to be effective.

A suggestion for practical work

This study has been derived from Exercise 16.2 suggested on page 306 of *Psychology: an Introduction*. It is an exercise in developing an attitude questionnaire.

You will need to pilot your draft questionnaire on several people in order to identify and correct its weaknesses.

Carrying out the study

STUDY

In planning your study, you will need to consider the following (consult Chapter 14, pages 246–51 and Chapter 22, pages 424–8 of *Psychology: an Introduction* if you need further explanation):

target population _____

test elements _____

test design and organisation _____

controls and precautions _____

sampling procedures _____

Ethical considerations _____

_____

_____

_____

_____

_____

Make notes on how you will carry out this study. _____

_____

_____

_____

Analysing the results

You will need to summarise the results obtained when you pilot the test. You will need a bar chart to display the results from your pilot sample visually. Consult Appendix 2B (page 205) for help in drawing this up. It should be called Fig. 1 and will need an appropriate title.

Reporting the study

You are now ready to write up your study in the correct format.

Use Checklist D in Appendix 3 (page 211) to make sure you have included everything you need to.

Sample examination question

Northern Examining Association, June 1990
Paper 2, Question 3
Paper reference: 2175

3   (a)   Read the following passage.

Both my wife and I have got good qualifications. I turned down a good job and accepted a slightly worse job in another town where my wife would have a better chance of getting a part-time job in her speciality. We bought a house near to my wife's work place so that she could pick the children up from school and get them their tea. Because my wife earns, she can afford to pay a cleaning lady to do her household chores. However, we try to share the other tasks around the house equally. For example, she cooks the meals, but I always do the washing up and ironing for her.

(i)   Explain the term "sex role stereotyping".

_____

_____   [3]

(ii)   Give **two** examples of sex role stereotyping from the above passage.

_____

_____   [2]

(b)   100 students were placed in one of two groups and asked to read the passages below.

Passage A

Permi left the class and made her way to the snack bar. On the way she waited for her friends. When she got to the snack bar, she decided to sit with some of her other friends whom she knew from the badminton club. They talked about one of the teachers who had just joined the club. After half an hour she left for her psychology lesson. Permi liked psychology because the teacher often split the class into small discussion groups and Permi liked to work in a team.

Passage B

When she left her class Permi decided to go to the library to do some work. As she made her way to it, she noticed some people she knew and decided to take a longer route in order to avoid talking to them. After completing the work she went to the snack bar for a short break. She sat down and drank her cup of tea by herself. When she had finished the cup of tea she left for her next class which was biology. Permi didn't like biology because the teacher made students work in groups.

The 50 students in Group I read passage B first and then passage A.

The 50 students in Group II read passage A first and then passage B.

After the reading had been completed all the students were asked to say whether they thought Permi was a friendly or unfriendly student. The bar chart above shows the results.

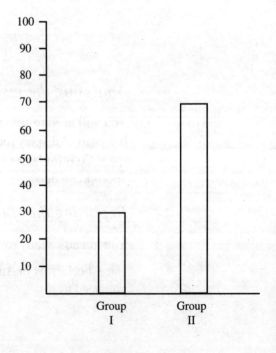

Use the bar chart to answer the following questions.

(i)   What percentage of Group I students rated Permi as **unfriendly**?

[1]

(ii) What can be concluded about Group II?

[1]

(iii) Explain why the differences between the two groups occurred.

[2]

(c)   Describe **one** other study concerned with impression formation.

[5]

(d)   You have applied for a job which involves working with elderly people. Explain **two** things that you could do at the interview to try to create the impression that you were the right person for the job. Use your knowledge of impression formation in your answer.

[6]

Chapter quiz

Answer the following questions in no longer than 10 minutes:

1   What do we call traits which appear to be very influential in forming impressions?

2   What name is given to the way that one or two positive traits can make other characteristics seem positive as well?

3   First impressions are also called   ?

4   Who showed that parents play differently with boy babies than with girl babies?

5   What name is given to our basic tendency to use dispositional rather than situational attributions, even if situational ones are appropriate?

6   What are the three factors involved in covariance?

7   Who provided students with rent-free accommodation in order to study friendship patterns?

8   What event did Walster arrange to study physical attraction?

9   What are the three components of an attitude?

10 Who set up rivalry between the Bulldogs and the Red Devils in order to study prejudice?

Chapter 17 – Communication

This chapter can be divided into two major segments, as follows:

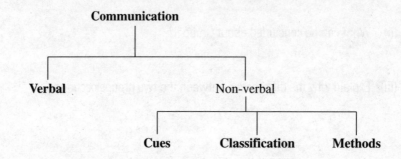

Each of those segments can then be subdivided into smaller tree diagrams. These can be useful in helping you to structure your revision.

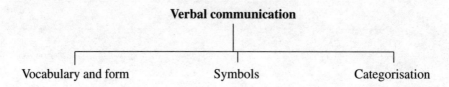

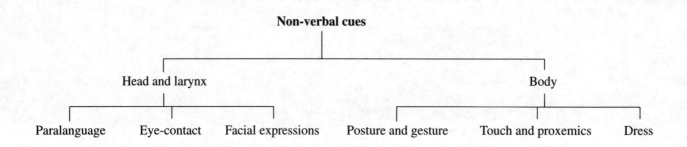

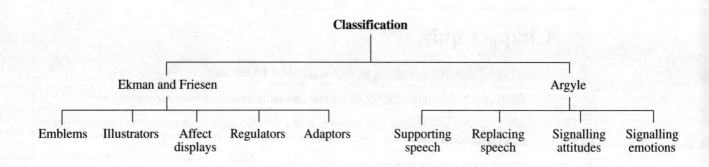

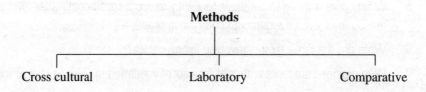

Planning an essay

When you are planning an essay for an examination, remember that you won't have enough time to write down everything you know about the subject. This means that the essay's structure is particularly important. You must bring in as much information that is relevant to the question as you can, and leave out extra or irrelevant details.

Even writing quite quickly, you will probably be able to write only one paragraph in five minutes, so your essay structure must be matched to the time you have available and you should plan what the paragraphs will cover with that in mind. Using this method, a 45-minute essay involves five minutes' thinking time and produces eight paragraphs. For example:

SAMPLE QUESTION

Giving experimental evidence, discuss the use of three of the following: paralanguage, eye-contact, facial expression, dress, proxemics.

Paragraph 1	introduction: verbal and non-verbal communication
Paragraph 2	eye-contact: Argyle and Dean's study
Paragraph 3	staring: Ellsworth's traffic study
Paragraph 4	facial expression: cross-cultural studies
Paragraph 5	Andrew: animal comparisons of facial expression
Paragraph 6	paralanguage and emotion: Kasl and Mahl
Paragraph 7	NVC and verbal information: Argyle, Alkema and Gilmour
Paragraph 8	conclusion: NVC is an important and complex part of social living

Try producing some essay outlines for yourself, using the following questions:

QUESTIONS

1   *Discuss the experimental study of eye-contact between human beings.*
2   *What can psychological research tell us about the non-verbal aspects of conversation?*
3   *What functions can non-verbal signals serve in human interaction?*
4   *Discuss the use of cross-cultural research in studying non-verbal communication.*

Question 1:	*Discuss the experimental study of eye-contact between human beings.*
Paragraph 1	introduction:
Paragraph 2	
Paragraph 3	
Paragraph 4	
Paragraph 5	
Paragraph 6	
Paragraph 7	
Paragraph 8	conclusion:
Question 2:	*What can psychological research tell us about the non-verbal aspects of conversation?*
Paragraph 1	introduction:
Paragraph 2	
Paragraph 3	

Paragraph 4

Paragraph 5

Paragraph 6

Paragraph 7

Paragraph 8   conclusion:

Question 3:   *What functions can non-verbal signals serve in human interaction?*

Paragraph 1   introduction:

Paragraph 2

Paragraph 3

Paragraph 4

Paragraph 5

Paragraph 6

Paragraph 7

Paragraph 8   conclusion:

Question 4:   *Discuss the use of cross-cultural research in studying non-verbal communication.*

Paragraph 1   introduction:

Paragraph 2

Paragraph 3

Paragraph 4

Paragraph 5

Paragraph 6

Paragraph 7

Paragraph 8   conclusion:

Chapter summary

(*Psychology: an Introduction*, page 336)

1   All social interaction involves some form of communication which may be verbal or non-verbal.

2   Verbal communication involves the use of language. It allows us to communicate symbolically and to refer to events or objects which are not present.

3   Non-verbal communication involves the use of a variety of cues to communicate information. Social interaction tends to involve a great deal of unconscious non-verbal communication.

4   There are eight main groups of non-verbal cues: paralanguage, eye contact, facial expression, posture, gesture, touch, proxemics and dress.

5   Ekman and Friesen classified non-verbal signals into five kinds: emblems, adapters, illustrators, affect displays and regulators. Each of these represents a different set of uses for the cues.

6   Non-verbal communication has been investigated through ethological or cross-cultural studies, laboratory studies and comparative studies.

Key sections for revision

1 types of communication
2 verbal communication
3 non-verbal communication
4 types of cues
5 functions of non-verbal signals
6 studying non-verbal communication

Issues and perspectives

Using the following table, note down any features of interest which relate to the key sections of the chapter.

Key section	Methods of study	Evaluation and criticism	Ethical issues
1 types of communication			
2 verbal communication			
3 non-verbal communication			
4 types of cues			
5 functions of non-verbal signals			
6 studying non-verbal communication			

Revision questions

Short-answer questions are useful for testing your knowledge of an area while you are revising, and for making sure that you understand it. They also often appear in examinations, and when they do you will have only a limited amount of time to answer them. The questions will be marked according to the information you have used to answer them and what you can attain marks for will be set out in a mark scheme.

Here are two 10-mark questions, with typical marking schemes which an examiner might use to assess answers.

Outline and discuss the functions of non-verbal communication identified by Argyle.

assisting speech	(up to)	2 marks
replacing speech	(up to)	2 marks
signalling attitudes	(up to)	2 marks
signalling emotions	(up to)	2 marks
evaluation/discussion	(up to)	2 marks
		Total 10 marks

Compare two studies of non-verbal communication which have used different methods of study.

description of first study	(up to)	3 marks
description of second study	(up to)	3 marks
comparison of methods used	(up to)	4 marks
		Total 10 marks

As you can see, each question has its own mark scheme and these share out the marks between the different types of knowledge needed to answer the question.

Bearing this in mind, try to work out your own mark schemes for each of the following questions. Each question is worth 10 marks. If you feel that you need more help, look at the mark schemes in the other chapters.

1   *Distinguish between verbal and non-verbal communication.*

2   *Outline three characteristics of verbal communication.*

3   *Describe and discuss a study of paralanguage in communication.*

4   *Briefly describe five different kinds of non-verbal cues.*

5   *What were the five functions of non-verbal cues identified by Ekman and Friesen.*

When you have written your mark scheme, turn to the relevant pages in your textbook and make sure that your scheme reflects the information covered by that topic.

Answering revision questions

Now try answering each of these questions, giving yourself 15 minutes to complete each one. At the end of that time, mark your answer, using the mark scheme that you have developed.

(NB: It is essential that you write the mark scheme <u>before</u> you try to answer the question! Doing it the other way round would be completely pointless because you would be too influenced by what you have already written.)

1   *Distinguish between verbal and non-verbal communication.*

2   *Outline three characteristics of verbal communication.*

3   *Describe and discuss a study of paralanguage in communication.*

4   *Briefly describe five different kinds of non-verbal cues.*

5   *What were the five functions of non-verbal cues identified by Ekman and Friesen.*

A suggestion for practical work

This study has been derived from Exercise 17.2 suggested on page 330 of *Psychology: an Introduction*. It is an experiment which will allow you to investigate personal space during conversation.

Carrying out the study

In planning your study, you will need to identify the following (consult Chapter 22, pages 424–8 of *Psychology: an Introduction* if you need further explanation):

hypothesis _____

null hypothesis _____

independent variable _____

dependent variable _____

design _____

controls _____

ethical considerations _____

_____

_____

_____

_____

_____

Make notes on how you will carry out this experiment. _____

_____

_____

_____

_____

Analysing the results

You will need a summary table of results which includes the mean, median and mode scores for your two conditions. It should be called Table 1 and will need a title telling your reader exactly what it is about. Consult Appendix 2A (page 205) for help in drawing up your table.

You will also need a diagram to display your findings visually. This will be called Fig. 1 and will take the form of a bar chart, showing the mean scores for each condition. Use the notes in Appendix 2B (page 205) to draw one up for your results.

Reporting the study

You are now ready to write up your experiment in the correct format.

Use Checklist A in the Appendix (page 210) to make sure you have included everything you need to.

Sample examination question

From: Taylor I. and Hayes N. (1990), *Investigating Psychology*, pages 111–12, Reading 5.5

Reading 5.5   *Gaze During Conversation*

It is found that glances are synchronised with speech in a special way. Kendon (1867) found that long glances were made, starting just before the end of an utterance, as shown by the graph, while the other person started to look away at this point.

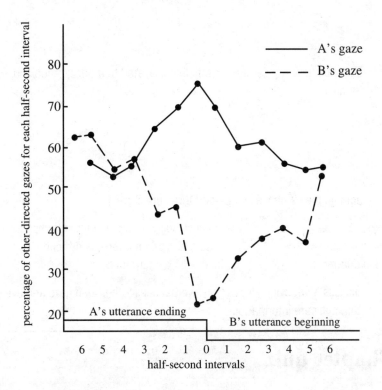

Direction of gaze at the beginning and end of long utterances.

The main reason why people look at the end of their utterances is that they need feedback on the other's response. This may be of various kinds. A wants to know whether B is still attending – his direction of gaze shows if he is asleep, or looking at someone else. A also wants to know how his last message was received – whether B understood, agreed, thought it was funny. At pauses in the middle of long speeches, A will look for continued permission to carry on speaking, and B will nod or grunt if he is agreeable to this.

In another experiment strong support was obtained for the hypothesis that looking is used to gain information on the other's response. Vision between A and B was interfered with in various ways, e.g. B wore (1) dark glasses, (2) a mask with only eyes showing, (3) was behind a one-way screen. In these conditions A was increasingly uncomfortable, was increasingly less clear about how B was reacting, and expressed a desire for more information about B's responses. The experiment shows that it is more useful to see the face than the eyes, though it was necessary to see the eyes themselves for signals about synchronising (Argyle, Lalljee and Cook, 1968).

In the Kendon study it was found that the terminal glance conveyed information to the other, that the speaker was about to stop speaking; if this glance were omitted, a long pause followed. In the one-way screen experiment there was much less gaze when subjects were asked to exchange monologues – where no signals for synchronising speech were required.

So gaze does three main jobs during conversation – it enables non-verbal reactions to be seen, it sends information, and it helps with synchronising of utterances.

M.Argyle (1979) *The Psychology of Interpersonal Behaviour* Penguin

1 a) When did Kendon (1967) find the speaker taking long looks in the conversation?

_____ [1]

 b) How does he explain this?

_____

_____ [2]

2 Describe the pattern of gaze made by A shown in the graph over the period of B's speech.

_____

_____ [2]

3 Describe how Argyle et al (1968) demonstrated that gaze, or looking, was necessary for feedback.

_____

_____

_____ [3]

4 Join up the sentences so that all three are correct:

gaze   unconsciously occurs when we find someone attractive
eye contact   occurs less when a topic is difficult
pupil dilation   increases with intimacy   [3]

5 Discuss, with evidence, two non-verbal cues (other than gaze and eye contact) which communicate information.   [8]

Chapter quiz

Answer the following questions in no longer than 10 minutes:

1 What is the name for communication which involves the use of words?

2 What characteristic of words allows us to use them to talk about things which are not present?

3 What is the general name for the other signals, apart from word-meaning, which are conveyed by spoken language?

4 Who studied patterns of eye-contact between pairs of students who were getting acquainted?

5 What unconscious feature of gaze signals attraction?

6 What aspect of facial expression is a signal of recognition all over the world?

7 Which technique uses electrical sensors to detect changes in the muscles of the face?

8 Who investigated conversational distances by asking businessmen and other professionals to have conversations with one another?

9 What two words are missing from this list: emblems, affect displays, adaptors.

10 Name the three main methods of studying non-verbal communication.

Chapter 18 – Social influences

This chapter can be divided into five major segments, as follows:

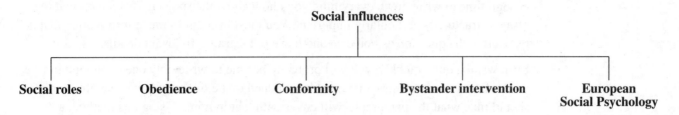

Social influences

Social roles   **Obedience**   **Conformity**   **Bystander intervention**   **European Social Psychology**

Each of those segments can then be subdivided into smaller tree diagrams. These can be useful in helping you to structure your revision.

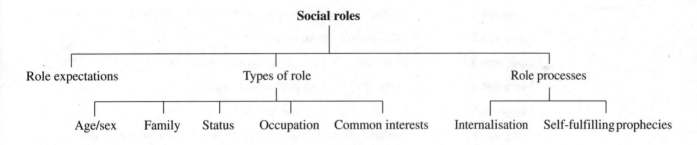

Social roles

Role expectations   Types of role   Role processes

Age/sex   Family   Status   Occupation   Common interests   Internalisation   Self-fulfilling prophecies

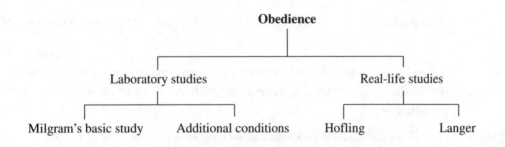

Obedience

Laboratory studies   Real-life studies

Milgram's basic study   Additional conditions   Hofling   Langer

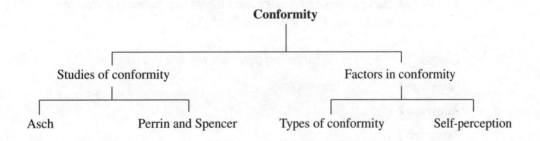

Conformity

Studies of conformity   Factors in conformity

Asch   Perrin and Spencer   Types of conformity   Self-perception

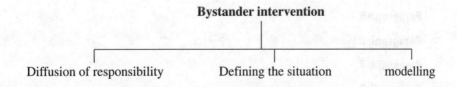

Bystander intervention

Diffusion of responsibility   Defining the situation   modelling

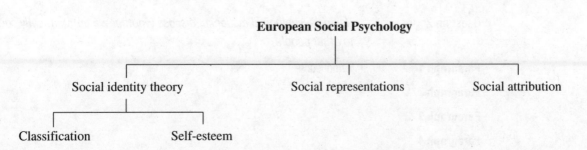

European Social Psychology

Social identity theory   Social representations   Social attribution

Classification   Self-esteem

Planning an essay

When you are planning an essay for an examination, remember that you won't have enough time to write down everything you know about the subject. This means that the essay's structure is particularly important. You must bring in as much information that is relevant to the question as you can, and leave out extra or irrelevant details.

Even writing quite quickly, you will probably be able to write only one paragraph in five minutes, so your essay structure must be matched to the time you have available and you should plan what the paragraphs will cover with that in mind. Using this method, a 45-minute essay involves five minutes' thinking time and produces eight paragraphs. For example:

SAMPLE QUESTION

How may the presence of other people affect our behaviour?

Paragraph 1	introduction: how psychologists have studied the effects of presence of others
Paragraph 2	coaction and audience effects
Paragraph 3	social roles, role expectations and social sanctions
Paragraph 4	conformity: brief description of Asch's study
Paragraph 5	Kelman's three types of conformity
Paragraph 6	obedience: the presence of the experimenter factor in Milgram's study
Paragraph 7	bystander intervention: diffusion of responsibility
Paragraph 8	conclusion: many different ways that the presence of others can influence us

Of course, this isn't the only way that you could answer this question. There are other possibilities. Try producing some essay outlines for yourself, using the following questions:

QUESTIONS

1   *What can psychologists tell us about obedience?*
2   *Using psychological evidence, discuss whether we automatically conform to other people*
3   *What factors can make us more or less likely to help someone in trouble?*
4   *Outline and describe European Social Psychology.*

Question 1:   *What can psychologists tell us about obedience?*

Paragraph 1   introduction:

Paragraph 2

Paragraph 3

Paragraph 4

Paragraph 5

Paragraph 6

Paragraph 7

Paragraph 8   conclusion:

Question 2:   *Using psychological evidence, discuss whether we automatically conform to other people*

Paragraph 1   introduction:

Paragraph 2

Paragraph 3

Paragraph 4

Paragraph 5

Paragraph 6

Paragraph 7

Paragraph 8   conclusion:

Question 3:   *What factors can make us more or less likely to help someone in trouble?*

Paragraph 1   introduction:

Paragraph 2

Paragraph 3

Paragraph 4

Paragraph 5

Paragraph 6

Paragraph 7

Paragraph 8   conclusion:

Question 4:   *Outline and describe European Social Psychology.*

Paragraph 1   introduction:

Paragraph 2

Paragraph 3

Paragraph 4

Paragraph 5

Paragraph 6

Paragraph 7

Paragraph 8   conclusion:

Chapter summary

(*Psychology: an Introduction*, pages 357–8)

1   Our behaviour is affected by the presence of other people in a number of different ways. Social roles are parts that we play in society. Any one person may be expected to play a variety of different roles in their everyday lives.

2   People have expectations about the behaviour that is appropriate for a particular role and may impose sanctions on those who do not conform.

3   Studies of obedience performed by Milgram and Hofling have shown that people will obey authority figures even when they think that what they are being asked to do is wrong.

4   Asch demonstrated that subjects would go along with the majority in a study involving judgements, even when they knew that the majority judgement was inaccurate.

5   Kelman proposed that there are three forms of conformity: compliance, identification and internalisation. Self-perception is also important in conformity.

6   Studies of bystander intervention have shown that diffusion of responsibility and defining the situation are important factors. If these do not apply then people are usually very helpful.

7   European Social Psychology is the name given to a group of theories which emphasise the importance of the wider social factors in society. It includes social identity theory, social representation theory and social attribution theory.

Key sections for revision

1 roles and groups
2 mechanisms of social roles
3 obedience
4 studies of conformity
5 features of conformity
6 bystander intervention
7 European Social Psychology

Issues and perspectives

Using the following table, note down any features of interest which relate to the key sections of the chapter.

Key section	Methods of study	Evaluation and criticism	Ethical issues
1 roles and groups			
2 mechanisms of social roles			
3 obedience			
4 studies of conformity			
5 features of conformity			
6 bystander intervention			
7 European Social Psychology			

Revision questions

Short-answer questions are useful for testing your knowledge of an area while you are revising, and for making sure that you understand it. They also often appear in examinations, and when they do you will have only a limited amount of time to answer them. The questions will be marked according to the information you have used to answer them and what you can attain marks for will be set out in a mark scheme.

Here are two 10-mark questions, with typical marking schemes which an examiner might use to assess answers.

How can role expectations affect us?

description of social role		1 mark
examples of social roles	(up to)	3 marks
description of role expectation	(up to)	3 marks
description of social sanctions	(up to)	3 marks
		Total 10 marks

Describe the five main types of social grouping.

names of the five groupings	(up to)	5 marks
an example of each grouping	(up to)	5 marks
		Total 10 marks

As you can see, each question has its own mark scheme and these share out the marks between the different types of knowledge needed to answer the question.

Bearing this in mind, try to work out your own mark schemes for each of the following questions. Each question is worth 10 marks. If you feel that you need more help, look at the mark schemes in the other chapters.

1   *Describe Hofling's experiment on obedience.*

2   *Discuss <u>one</u> criticism of Asch's experiment.*

3   *What is meant by the term conformity?*

4   *Describe <u>one</u> factor which may influence bystander intervention.*

5   *How may social representations change?*

When you have written your mark scheme, turn to the relevant pages in your textbook and make sure that your scheme reflects the information covered by that topic.

Answering revision questions

Now try answering each of these questions, giving yourself 15 minutes to complete each one. At the end of that time, mark your answer, using the mark scheme that you have developed.

(NB: It is essential that you write the mark scheme <u>before</u> you try to answer the question! Doing it the other way round would be completely pointless because you would be too influenced by what you have already written.)

1   *Describe Hofling's experiment on obedience.*

2   *Discuss <u>one</u> criticism of Asch's experiment.*

3   *What is meant by the term conformity?*

4   *Describe <u>one</u> factor which may influence bystander intervention.*

5   *How may social representations change?*

A suggestion for practical work

This study has been derived from Exercise 18.1 suggested on page 338 of *Psychology: an Introduction*. It is a correlation study which will allow you to look at the relationship between age and social roles.

It has been suggested that adults tend to have more social roles than people who are still at school. You could undertake a study which involved asking people to identify the number of social roles they play, and correlating that information with their age.

Carrying out the study

In planning your study, you will need to identify the following (consult Chapter 22, pages 424–8 of *Psychology: an Introduction* if you need further explanation):

hypothesis

null hypothesis

variable 1

variable 2

controls

ethical considerations

Make notes on how you will carry out this research.

Analysing the results

You will need a diagram to display your findings visually. This should be called Fig. 1, and in this case it will be a scattergram. Use the notes in Appendix 2D (page 208) to help you to draw this up.

Reporting the study

You are now ready to write up your experiment in the correct format.

Use Checklist B in Appendix 3 (page 210) to make sure you have included everything you need to.

Sample examination questions

Midlands Examining Group, June 1990
Social Module,   Source A, Questions 1/4
Paper reference: 755

I'm in with the In-Crowd

In the classic conformity experiment by Asch, subjects were sat around a table and asked in turn to say which line from card A was the same length as the line on card B.

Card A | | | | Card B

Only one of the people at the table was a subject, the rest were confederates (stooges) of the experimenter. The confederates would all give the wrong answer, and Asch wanted to know how many of the subjects would conform to the others and also give the wrong answer. The crosses represent seats at the table, and the numbers represent the order in which the people are asked to answer.

```
        3        4        5
        ×        ×        ×
   2 ×  ┌──────────────────┐  × 6
        │      TABLE        │
   1 ×  └──────────────────┘  × 7
```

1   What number chair would you put the subject in to get the greatest conformity?

_____ [1]

2   In a variation of the experiment, the confederate who was sitting in chair 2 did not agree with the majority. What effect do you think this had on the subject who was sitting in chair 4?

_____ [1]

3   Describe another study on conformity.

_____

_____

_____

_____ [4]

4   Not all subjects conform to the majority. Give **three** factors that would make people *more* likely to conform in your experiment or the Asch experiment.

Factor 1:

_____

Factor 2:

_____

Factor 3:

_____ [3]

Chapter quiz

Answer the following questions in no longer than 10 minutes:

1   What is the name for the punishments and controls used by society to make sure that people conform to role expectations?

2   What level of obedience did Milgram find when he conducted his research in an office block in the city?

3   In Hofling's study of obedience, _____ were asked to administer a dangerous dose of a drug called Astroten.

4   Who argued that Asch's research into conformity was 'a child of its time'?

5   Which is the odd one out: compliance, internalisation, identification, imitation?

6   What proportion of people reported smoke pouring from a ventilator grille when they were waiting by themselves?

7   What term is used to describe the way that people did not help out when there were others around, on the grounds that they could help just as easily?

8   Which two psychologists developed social identity theory?

9   The shared social beliefs which occur in everyday life are known as _____ .

10 Which ethnic groups did Taylor and Jaggi study in their research into social attribution?

Chapter 19 – The social-learning approach to child development

This chapter can be divided into three major segments, as follows:

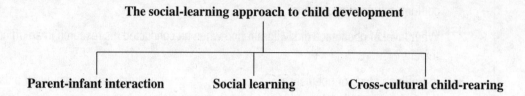

Each of those segments can then be subdivided into smaller tree diagrams. These can be useful in helping you to structure your revision.

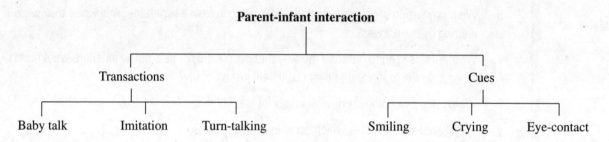

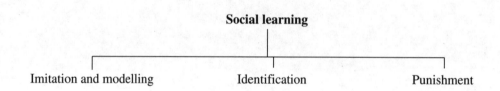

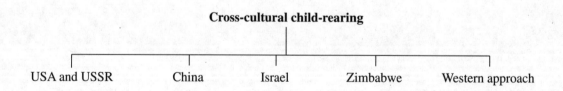

Planning an essay

When you are planning an essay for an examination, remember that you won't have enough time to write down everything you know about the subject. This means that the essay's structure is particularly important. You must bring in as much information that is relevant to the question as you can, and leave out extra or irrelevant details.

Even writing quite quickly, you will probably be able to write only one paragraph in five minutes, so your essay structure must be matched to the time you have available and you should plan what the paragraphs will cover with that in mind. Using this method, a 45-minute essay involves five minutes' thinking time and produces eight paragraphs. For example:

SAMPLE QUESTION

How does social learning theory contribute to our understanding of child development?

Paragraph 1   introduction: social learning as alternative to behaviourism

Paragraph 2   social interaction from early infancy

Paragraph 3   infant eye-contact and imitation

Paragraph 4   imitation: aggression study

Paragraph 5   parents modelling behaviours for children

Paragraph 6   the process of identification

Paragraph 7   influence of parents, media role models, etc.

Paragraph 8   conclusion: social learning important in development

Of course, this isn't the only possible way of tackling this question. Try producing some essay outlines for yourself, using the following questions:

QUESTIONS

1   *What are the main mechanisms involved in parent-infant interaction?*
2   *Using psychological evidence, discuss the importance of imitation and identification in child development.*
3   *What have psychologists discovered about the use of rewards and punishments to influence children?*
4   *Compare and contrast <u>three</u> different cultural child-rearing styles.*

Question 1:   *What are the main mechanisms involved in parent-infant interaction?*

Paragraph 1   introduction:

Paragraph 2

Paragraph 3

Paragraph 4

Paragraph 5

Paragraph 6

Paragraph 7

Paragraph 8   conclusion:

Question 2:   *Using psychological evidence, discuss the importance of imitation and identification in child development.*

Paragraph 1   introduction:

Paragraph 2

Paragraph 3

Paragraph 4

Paragraph 5

Paragraph 6

Paragraph 7

Paragraph 8   conclusion:

Question 3:   *What have psychologists discovered about the use of rewards and punishments to influence children?*

Paragraph 1   introduction:

Paragraph 2

Paragraph 3

Paragraph 4

Paragraph 5

Paragraph 6

Paragraph 7

Paragraph 8   conclusion:

Question 4:   *Compare and contrast <u>three</u> different cultural child-rearing styles.*

Paragraph 1   introduction:

Paragraph 2

Paragraph 3

Paragraph 4

Paragraph 5

Paragraph 6

Paragraph 7

Paragraph 8   conclusion:

Chapter summary

(*Psychology: an Introduction*, page 387)

1 Attachments between parents and infants develop through a process of interaction between the infant and its caretaker from the very first weeks of life.

2 Infants and parents interact using a variety of non-verbal signals which are thought to set the basis for future social contacts.

3 Imitation is a major method of learning for children, allowing them to pick up sequences of behaviour quickly and efficiently.

4 Identification is a longer-term process, by which a child may come to internalise the values and role-behaviour of a role-model.

5 The types of punishment used by parents may affect the likelihood of a child developing a strong conscience in later life.

6 Different societies have different ideas about child-rearing. Social influences on children in the former USSR are more consistent than in the USA.

7 Many cultures emphasise that the child is primarily a member of society and direct their child-rearing practices accordingly.

Key sections for revision

1 parent-infant interaction
2 interactional cues
3 imitation
4 identification
5 reward and punishment
6 American and Russian child-rearing
7 child-rearing in other cultures

Issues and perspectives

Using the following table, note down any features of interest which relate to the key sections of the chapter.

Key section	Methods of study	Evaluation and criticism	Ethical issues
1 parent-infant interaction			
2 interactional cues			
3 imitation			
4 identification			
5 reward and punishment			
6 American and Russian child-rearing			
7 child-rearing in other cultures			

Revision questions

Short-answer questions are useful for testing your knowledge of an area while you are revising, and for making sure that you understand it. They also often appear in examinations, and when they do you will have only a limited amount of time to answer them. The questions will be marked according to the information you have used to answer them and what you can attain marks for will be set out in a mark scheme.

Here are two 10-mark questions, with typical marking schemes which an examiner might use to assess answers.

What non-verbal signals does the infant have available for communication?

infant predisposition to sociability		1 mark
smiling in response to stimuli	(up to)	3 marks
crying: different messages	(up to)	3 marks
eye-contact: developing preferences	(up to)	3 marks
		Total 10 marks

Compare and contrast Bronfenbrenner's observations of child-rearing in the USA and USSR.

description of US practices	(up to)	2 marks
description of USSR practices	(up to)	2 marks
similarities	(up to)	2 marks
differences	(up to)	2 marks
evaluation of study	(up to)	2 marks
		Total 10 marks

As you can see, each question has its own mark scheme and these share out the marks between the different types of knowledge needed to answer the question.

Bearing this in mind, try to work out your own mark schemes for each of the following questions. Each question is worth 10 marks. If you feel that you need more help, look at the mark schemes in the other chapters.

1   *Describe <u>three</u> ways that parents and infants interact with one another.*

2   *Describe and discuss a study of imitation.*

3   *What is meant by the term 'identification'? Give a specific example.*

4   *How may punishment influence the development of conscience?*

5   *Describe and discuss child-rearing in a traditional culture in Zimbabwe.*

When you have written your mark scheme, turn to the relevant pages in your textbook and make sure that your scheme reflects the information covered by that topic.

Answering revision questions

Now try answering each of these questions, giving yourself 15 minutes to complete each one. At the end of that time, mark your answer, using the mark scheme that you have developed.

(NB: It is essential that you write the mark scheme <u>before</u> you try to answer the question! Doing it the other way round would be completely pointless because you would be too influenced by what you have already written.)

QUESTIONS   1   *Describe <u>three</u> ways that parents and infants interact with one another.*

2   *Describe and discuss a study of imitation.*

3   *What is meant by the term 'identification'? Give a specific example.*

4   *How may punishment influence the development of conscience?*

5   *Describe and discuss child-rearing in a traditional culture in Zimbabwe.*

A suggestion for practical work

This study has been derived from Exercise 19.1 suggested on page 367 of *Psychology: an Introduction*. This is an observational study which will allow you to look at the process of observing human interaction in a systematic way.

Carrying out the study

In planning your study, you will need to identify the following (consult Chapter 22, pages 424–8 of *Psychology: an Introduction* if you need further explanation):

hypothesis _____

null hypothesis _____

behaviours to be observed _____

design _____

controls _____

ethical considerations _____

_____

_____

_____

_____

_____

Make notes on how you will carry out this observation. _____

_____

_____

_____

_____

Analysing the results

You will need a summary table of results giving the frequency of occurence of behaviours that have been observed. It should be called Table 1 and will need an appropriate title. Consult Appendix 2A (page 205) for help in drawing up a table.

You will also need a bar chart to display your results visually. The bar chart will be called Fig. 1 and will show the categories of behaviour that you have observed and how often they occurred. Use one bar for each different behaviour. Consult Appendix 2B (page 205) if you feel that you need help in drawing up your bar chart.

Reporting the study

You are now ready to write up your observation in the correct format.

Use Checklist C in Appendix 3 (page 211) to make sure you have included everything you need to.

Sample examination question

Northern Examining Association, June 1991
Paper 2, Question 2
Paper reference: 2175

2   A study investigated the television habits and aggressiveness of 8 children. Information was collected about the amount of violence each child watched on television each week. Observers rated each child's aggressiveness on a scale of 0 to 10. The ratings were plotted as a scattergram.

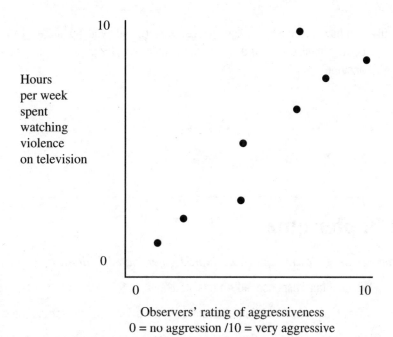

Hours per week spent watching violence on television

Observers' rating of aggressiveness
0 = no aggression /10 = very aggressive

(a)   Describe the findings in words.

_____

_____   [2]

(b)   What type of correlation is shown in the scattergram? Tick the correct box.

Positive correlation   ☐

Negative correlation   ☐

Zero correlation   ☐   [1]

(c)   Explain why it would be wrong to conclude from this study that these children's aggressiveness was **caused** by watching television violence.

_____

_____

_____   [3]

(d)   Describe any **one** study which shows that adults behave differently towards boys compared with how they behave towards girls.

_____

_____

_____   [5]

(e)   What is meant by the term socialisation?

_____

_____

_____   [3]

(f)   Explain how socialisation is demonstrated in the study you have described in (d) above.

_____

_____

_____   [3]

(g)   You have taken a job which involves working with young children. Explain **one** thing you could do to minimize sex stereotyping in the children. Use psychological theory to support your answer.

_____

_____

_____   [3]

Chapter quiz

Answer the following questions in no longer than 10 minutes:

1   Which infant response did Ahrens study?

2   What type of parent-infant interaction helps infants to understand the words in a language?

3   Who showed that the timing of parent-infant turn-taking is similar to that in adult conversation?

4   What type of baby will turn its head away when it is spoken to?

5   Which reflex involves the infant flinging its arms wide then bringing them together on its chest?

6   Which mechanism is sometimes described as 'a short-cut to learning'?

7   What apparatus did Bandura use to study aggressive learning in children?

8   Which two types of punishment were investigated by Mackinnon?

9   Who studied child-rearing in China?

10   In a traditional Shona family, who looks after the toddler?

This chapter can be divided into two major segments, as follows:

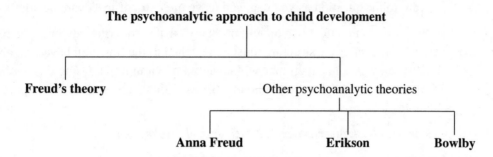

The psychoanalytic approach to child development

Freud's theory   Other psychoanalytic theories

Anna Freud   **Erikson**   **Bowlby**

Each of those segments can then be subdivided into smaller tree diagrams. These can be useful in helping you to structure your revision.

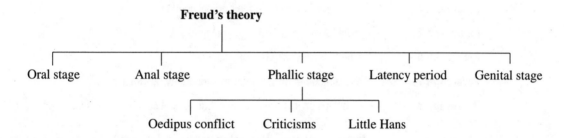

Freud's theory

Oral stage   Anal stage   Phallic stage   Latency period   Genital stage

Oedipus conflict   Criticisms   Little Hans

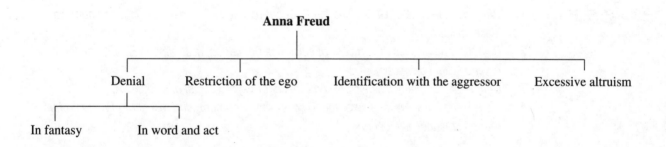

Anna Freud

Denial   Restriction of the ego   Identification with the aggressor   Excessive altruism

In fantasy   In word and act

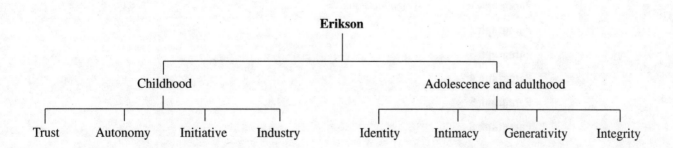

Erikson

Childhood   Adolescence and adulthood

Trust   Autonomy   Initiative   Industry   Identity   Intimacy   Generativity   Integrity

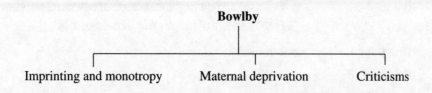

Bowlby

Imprinting and monotropy   Maternal deprivation   Criticisms

Planning an essay

When you are planning an essay for an examination, remember that you won't have enough time to write down everything you know about the subject. This means that the essay's structure is particularly important. You must bring in as much information that is relevant to the question as you can, and leave out extra or irrelevant details.

Even writing quite quickly, you will probably be able to write only one paragraph in five minutes, so your essay structure must be matched to the time you have available and you should plan what the paragraphs will cover with that in mind. Using this method, a 45-minute essay involves five minutes' thinking time and produces eight paragraphs. For example:

SAMPLE QUESTION

Outline and discuss the Freudian approach to child development.

Paragraph 1	introduction: the concept of libido
Paragraph 2	the oral stage
Paragraph 3	the anal stage
Paragraph 4	the phallic stage and the Oedipal conflict
Paragraph 5	the latency period/the genital stage
Paragraph 6	problem: Freud's view of evidence
Paragraph 7	finding other evidence for the continuity hypothesis
Paragraph 8	conclusion: may have validity but doesn't conform to normal scientific criteria

Of course, this isn't the only way of doing this essay and if you have other views you may wish to approach the discussion quite differently. Try producing some essay outlines for yourself, using the following questions:

1 *What can the case of Little Hans tell us about psycho-sexual development and defence mechanisms?*
2 *Describe and discuss the process of sexual identification, according to Freud's theory of psycho-sexual development.*
3 *Outline and critically discuss Erikson's theory of psycho-social development.*
4 *'That Freud has a lot to answer for.' Discuss this sentiment with respect to Western child-rearing practices and beliefs.*

Question 1:	*What can the case of Little Hans tell us about psycho-sexual development and defence mechanisms?*
Paragraph 1	introduction:
Paragraph 2	
Paragraph 3	
Paragraph 4	
Paragraph 5	
Paragraph 6	
Paragraph 7	
Paragraph 8	conclusion:

Question 2:	*Describe and discuss the process of sexual identification, according to Freud's theory of psycho-sexual development.*
Paragraph 1	introduction:
Paragraph 2	

Paragraph 3

Paragraph 4

Paragraph 5

Paragraph 6

Paragraph 7

Paragraph 8   conclusion:

Question 3:   *Outline and critically discuss Erikson's theory of psycho-social development.*

Paragraph 1   introduction:

Paragraph 2

Paragraph 3

Paragraph 4

Paragraph 5

Paragraph 6

Paragraph 7

Paragraph 8   conclusion:

Question 4:   *'That Freud has a lot to answer for.' Discuss this sentiment with respect to Western child-rearing practices and beliefs.*

Paragraph 1   introduction:

Paragraph 2

Paragraph 3

Paragraph 4

Paragraph 5

Paragraph 6

Paragraph 7

Paragraph 8   conclusion:

Chapter summary

(*Psychology: an Introduction*, page 399)

1   Freud considered that people were often influenced by unconscious wishes and by emotional traumas laid down in childhood.

2   He considered that the child passed through five psycho-sexual stages: oral, anal, phallic, latency and genital. The first three stages were important in determining later personality.

3   In the third stage, the child is faced with the resolution of either the Oedipus complex or the penis envy complex, which would determine sex-role identification.

4   Freud's study of Little Hans illustrated his ideas on how the Oedipus complex could provide traumas and how it could be resolved.

5   Anna Freud continued Freud's ideas, investigating the use of ego-defence mechanisms in children.

6   Erikson, a post-Freudian, developed a theory of eight psycho-social conflicts which needed resolution at stages throughout the whole of an individual's life.

7   Bowlby's theory of maternal deprivation arose from the psychoanalytic idea of the early years being all-important in development.

Key sections for revision

1   the unconscious mind
2   psycho-sexual stages
3   the Oedipal conflict
4   Little Hans
5   ego-defence mechanisms
6   Erikson's 'whole-life' theory
7   maternal deprivation theory

Issues and perspectives

Using the following table, note down any features of interest which relate to the key sections of the chapter.

Key section	Methods of study	Evaluation and criticism	Ethical issues
1 the unconscious mind			
2 psycho-sexual stages			
3 the Oedipal conflict			
4 Little Hans			
5 ego-defence mechanisms			
6 Erikson's 'whole-life' theory			
7 maternal deprivation theory			

Revision questions

Short-answer questions are useful for testing your knowledge of an area while you are revising, and for making sure that you understand it. They also often appear in examinations, and when they do you will have only a limited amount of time to answer them. The questions will be marked according to the information you have used to answer them and what you can attain marks for will be set out in a mark scheme.

Here are two 10-mark questions, with typical marking schemes which an examiner might use to assess answers.

Critically evaluate Freud's concept of the Oedipus conflict.

concept of libido		1 mark
phallic stage of development	(up to)	2 marks
description of Oedipus conflict	(up to)	2 marks
criticisms (at least 3 criticisms for all 5 marks)	(up to)	5 marks
		Total 10 marks

What were the ego-defence mechanisms identified by Anna Freud?

definition of ego-defence mechanisms		1 mark
denial in fantasy	(up to)	2 marks
denial in word and act	(up to)	2 marks
restriction of the ego	(up to)	2 marks
identification with the aggressor	(up to)	2 marks
excessive altruism	(up to)	1 mark
		Total 10 marks

As you can see, each question has its own mark scheme and these share out the marks between the different types of knowledge needed to answer the question.

Bearing this in mind, try to work out your own mark schemes for each of the following questions. Each question is worth 10 marks. If you feel that you need more help, look at the mark schemes in the other chapters.

1   *How did Freud obtain evidence for his theory?*

2   *List the five psycho-sexual stages outlined by Freud.*

3   *Describe and evaluate the psychoanalytic explanation for the case of Little Hans.*

4   *Contrast Erikson's and Freud's theories of development.*

5   *What was the theoretical basis of Bowlby's ideas about maternal deprivation?*

When you have written your mark scheme, turn to the relevant pages in your textbook and make sure that your scheme reflects the information covered by that topic.

Answering revision questions

Now try answering each of these questions, giving yourself 15 minutes to complete each one. At the end of that time, mark your answer, using the mark scheme that you have developed.

(NB: It is essential that you write the mark scheme <u>before</u> you try to answer the question! Doing it the other way round would be completely pointless because you would be too influenced by what you have already written.)

 **QUESTIONS**

1   *How did Freud obtain evidence for his theory?*

2   *List the five psycho-sexual stages outlined by Freud.*

3   *Describe and evaluate the psychoanalytic explanation for the case of Little Hans.*

4   *Contrast Erikson's and Freud's theories of development.*

5   *What was the theoretical basis of Bowlby's ideas about maternal deprivation?*

A suggestion for practical work

This study has been derived from Exercise 20.1 suggested on page 254 of *Psychology: an Introduction*. It is an exercise in developing a psychometric test based on free association.

Begin by developing a list of a large number of words which older and younger people might be likely to use or react to differently (for instance, 'acid', 'hippy', DJ, etc.) Pilot this list on several people of different ages. From the outcome of the pilot test, select for your final list the words that seem to produce the most difference between age groups.

Carrying out the study

In planning your study, you will need to identify the following (consult Chapter 14, pages 246–51 and Chapter 22, pages 424–8 of *Psychology: an Introduction* if you need further explanation):

target population _____

test elements _____

test design and organisation _____

controls and precautions _____

sampling procedures _____

ethical considerations _____

_____

_____

_____

_____

_____

Make notes on how you will go about developing this test. _____

_____

_____

_____

_____

Analysing the results

You will need to summarise the results obtained when you pilot the test. Once you have organised the answers into categories, you can use bar charts to display the results of your pilot sample visually. Consult Appendix 2B (page 205) for help in drawing this up. It should be called Fig. 1 and will need an appropriate title.

Reporting the study

You are now ready to write up your study in the correct format.

Use Checklist D in Appendix 3 (page 211) to make sure you have included everything you need to.

Sample examination questions

Northern Examinations and Assessment Board, June 1993
Paper 2, Question 1
Paper reference: 2415

Answer **all six** questions

1   The graph shows children's requests for toys in letters to Father Christmas.

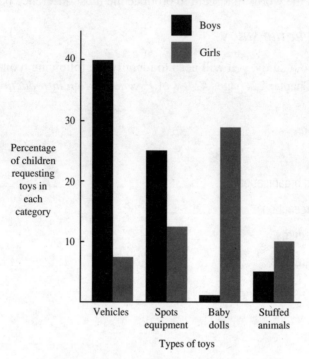

(a)   For which toy was there the **greatest** difference in requests between girls and boys?

_____   [1]

(b)   For which toy was there the **smallest** difference in requests between girls and boys?

_____   [1]

(c)   (i)   Describe "imitation" and explain how it might have lead to the differences in requests for baby dolls.

_____

_____

_____   [3]

(ii)   Describe "positive reinforcement" and explain how it might have lead to the differences in requests for vehicles.

_____

_____

_____   [3]

(d)   Describe how Freud believed sex-role behaviour develops in **boys**.

_____

_____

_____

_____   [5]

(e)   Briefly describe evidence Freud used to support his theory about the development of sex-role behaviour.

_____

_____

_____   [3]

(f)   Give **two** reasons why psychologists have disagreed with the work of Freud.

(i)   Reason 1

_____

_____   [2]

(ii)   Reason 2

_____

_____   [2]

Chapter quiz

Answer the following questions in no longer than 10 minutes:

1   Which <u>two</u> stages are missing from this list: oral, latency, genital?

2   According to Freud, what psychological characteristic would result from strict potty-training, producing a mean, grasping adult?

3   According to Freud, during which stage does a young boy experience the Oedipus conflict?

4   What is the name of the particular anxiety produced by the Oedipus conflict?

5   Who became frightened of horses when he was four years old?

6   What aspect of the child's psychology did Anna Freud concentrate on?

7   In Erikson's theory, at what time of life would someone need to resolve the conflict of identity versus role-confusion?

8   According to Erikson, which psycho-social conflict has to be resolved in maturity?

9   Who studied psychological recovery in later childhood?

10   On which feature of animal behaviour did Bowlby base his ideas of maternal deprivation?

Chapter 21 – The structuralist approach to child development

This chapter can be divided into two major segments, as follows:

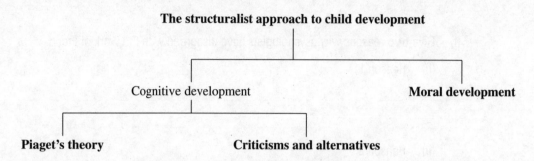

Each of those segments can then be subdivided into smaller tree diagrams. These can be useful in helping you to structure your revision.

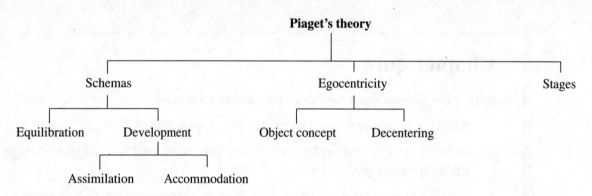

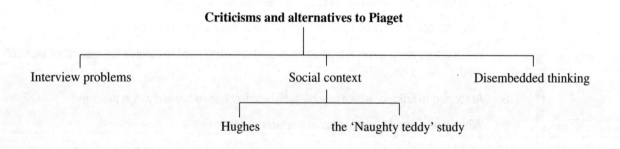

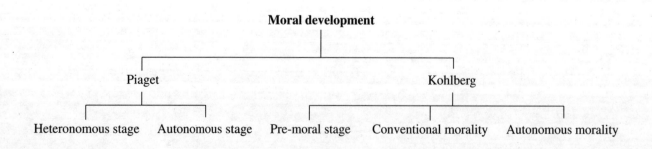

Planning an essay

When you are planning an essay for an examination, remember that you won't have enough time to write down everything you know about the subject. This means that the essay's structure is particularly important. You must bring in as much information that is relevant to the question as you can, and leave out extra or irrelevant details.

Even writing quite quickly, you will probably be able to write only one paragraph in five minutes, so your essay structure must be matched to the time you have available and you should plan what the paragraphs will cover with that in mind. Using this method, a 45-minute essay involves five minutes' thinking time and produces eight paragraphs. For example:

SAMPLE QUESTION

Critically discuss Piaget's theory of child development.

Paragraph 1	introduction: cognitive development in stages
Paragraph 2	forming schemas: assimilation and accommodation
Paragraph 3	the body-schema; reduction of egocentricity
Paragraph 4	the sensori-motor and pre-operational stages
Paragraph 5	the concrete and formal operational stages
Paragraph 6	recent studies: egocentricity and conservation
Paragraph 7	criticisms of Piagetian approach
Paragraph 8	conclusion: may have neglected social factors

Of course, this isn't the only possible way of tackling this question. Try producing some essay outlines for yourself, using the following questions:

1 *According to Piaget, the formation of schemas is the basis of all cognitive development. How does schema-formation change as the child grows older.*
2 *Describe and critically evaluate the Piagetian concept of egocentricity.*
3 *In your opinion, what re-evaluations of Piaget's theory are needed in the light of recent experimental evidence?*
4 *Compare and contrast Piaget's and Kohlberg's theories of moral development.*

Question 1: *According to Piaget, the formation of schemas is the basis of all cognitive development. How does schema-formation change as the child grows older?*

Paragraph 1	introduction:
Paragraph 2	
Paragraph 3	
Paragraph 4	
Paragraph 5	
Paragraph 6	
Paragraph 7	
Paragraph 8	conclusion:

Question 2: *Describe and critically evaluate the Piagetian concept of egocentricity.*

Paragraph 1	introduction:
Paragraph 2	
Paragraph 3	

Paragraph 4

Paragraph 5

Paragraph 6

Paragraph 7

Paragraph 8   conclusion:

Question 3:   *In your opinion, what re-evaluations of Piaget's theory are needed in the light of recent experimental evidence?*

Paragraph 1   introduction:

Paragraph 2

Paragraph 3

Paragraph 4

Paragraph 5

Paragraph 6

Paragraph 7

Paragraph 8   conclusion:

Question 4:   *Compare and contrast Piaget's and Kohlberg's theories of moral development.*

Paragraph 1   introduction:

Paragraph 2

Paragraph 3

Paragraph 4

Paragraph 5

Paragraph 6

Paragraph 7

Paragraph 8   conclusion:

Chapter summary

(*Psychology: an Introduction*, page 417)

1   Piaget suggested that cognitive development happened through the formation of schemata.
2   Egocentricity is reduced through the development of the body-schema, the object-concept, and the ability to 'decentre'.
3   Piaget identified four stages of cognitive development: the sensori-motor stage, the pre-operational stage, the concrete operational stage and the formal operational stage.
4   Critics of Piaget have argued that his tasks were too artificial to test children's real cognitive abilities, and have also criticised the way that he carried out his studies.
5   Many modern researchers consider that social cognition is a more relevant approach to intellectual development than Piaget's theory.
6   Piaget's theory of moral development was that children progressed from a 'heteronomous' stage to an 'autonomous' stage as they matured.
7   Kohlberg identified three stages of moral development: the pre-moral stage and the stages of conventional morality and autonomous morality.

Key sections for revision

1 schema-formation
2 egocentricity
3 stages of cognitive development
4 criticisms of Piaget
5 alternative approaches
6 Piaget's theory of moral development
7 Kohlberg's theory of moral development

Issues and perspectives

Using the following table, note down any features of interest which relate to the key sections of the chapter.

Key section	Methods of study	Evaluation and criticism	Ethical issues
1 schema-formation			
2 egocentricity			
3 sages of cognitive development			
4 criticisms of Piaget			
5 alternative approaches			
6 Piaget's theory of moral development			
7 Kohlberg's theory of moral development			

Revision questions

Short-answer questions are useful for testing your knowledge of an area while you are revising, and for making sure that you understand it. They also often appear in examinations, and when they do you will have only a limited amount of time to answer them. The questions will be marked according to the information you have used to answer them and what you can attain marks for will be set out in a mark scheme.

Here are two 10-mark questions, with typical marking schemes which an examiner might use to assess answers.

Outline Piaget's stages of cognitive development.

schemas		1 mark
sensori-motor stage	(up to)	2 marks
pre-operational	(up to)	3 marks
concrete operational	(up to)	2 marks
formal operational	(up to)	2 marks
		Total 10 marks

How did Piaget study moral development in children?

clinical interviews	(up to)	2 marks
explaining rules of marbles	(up to)	3 marks
judgements about examples	(up to)	3 marks
nature of judgements	(up to)	2 marks
		Total 10 marks

As you can see, each question has its own mark scheme and these share out the marks between the different types of knowledge needed to answer the question.

Bearing this in mind, try to work out your own mark schemes for each of the following questions. Each question is worth 10 marks. If you feel that you need more help, look at the mark schemes in the other chapters.

1   *How are schemas formed?*

2   *Give two examples of the reduction of egocentricity through infancy and childhood.*

3   *Describe and discuss a study which challenges Piagetian ideas of cognitive development.*

4   *What is meant by social cognition in child development? Give examples.*

5   *What were Kohlberg's three stages of moral development?*

When you have written your mark scheme, turn to the relevant pages in your textbook and make sure that your scheme reflects the information covered by that topic.

Answering revision questions

Now try answering each of these questions, giving yourself 15 minutes to complete each one. At the end of that time, mark your answer, using the mark scheme that you have developed.

(NB: It is essential that you write the mark scheme before you try to answer the question! Doing it the other way round would be completely pointless because you would be too influenced by what you have already written.)

1   *How are schemas formed?*

2   *Give <u>two</u> examples of the reduction of egocentricity through infancy and childhood.*

3   *Describe and discuss a study which challenges Piagetian ideas of cognitive development.*

4   *What is meant by social cognition in child development? Give examples.*

5   *What were Kohlberg's three stages of moral development?*

A suggestion for practical work

This study has been derived from Exercise 21.1 suggested on pages 410–11 of *Psychology: an Introduction*. It is an experiment which will allow you to explore the types of concepts which older and younger children form.

Carrying out the study

In planning your study, you will need to identify the following (consult Chapter 22, pages 424–8 of *Psychology: an Introduction* if you need further explanation):

hypothesis _____

null hypothesis _____

independent variable _____

dependent variable _____

design _____

controls _____

ethical considerations _____

_____

_____

_____

_____

_____

Make notes on how you will carry out this study. _____

_____

_____

_____

_____

Analysing the results

You will need a summary table of results which gives the number of responses in each category for each of the two age groups. It should be called Table 1 and will need a title telling your reader exactly what it is about. Consult Appendix 2A (page 205) for help in drawing up your table.

You will also need a diagram to display your findings visually. This should be called Fig. 1 and should be a bar chart. One of the bars will represent the younger group and the other will represent the older group. Consult Appendix 2B (page 205) for help in drawing this up.

Reporting the study

You are now ready to write up your experiment in the correct format.

Use Checklist A in Appendix 3 (page 210) to make sure you have included everything you need to.

Sample examination questions

> Midlands Examining Group, February 1989
> Developmental I Module, Source B, Questions 5/9
> Paper reference: 678

Understanding Conversation

Michael (aged 5): 'Mum, may Patrick and I have a drink?'
Mum: 'Okay. Could you both come into the kitchen and I'll get it for you?'
Michael: 'Aw, Mum. You've poured the juice into the wrong cups. I want my special glass from McDonalds.'
Mum: 'Oh, okay. (The children watch as she pours Michael's juice from the cup into a long, thin glass.)

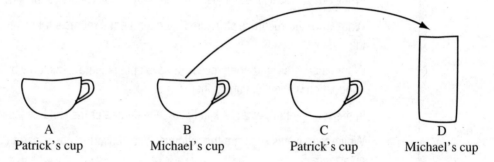

| A | B | C | D |
| Patrick's cup | Michael's cup | Patrick's cup | Michael's cup |

Michael: 'Look Mum, it's not fair now. I've got more drink than Patrick.'
Patrick (aged 7): 'No you haven't, it just looks like more.'
Mum: 'Patrick is right. I've got two different glasses but the amount of drink is still the same.'
Michael: 'I see what you mean now. The long thin glass just makes it look like there is more drink in it. So it is fair. Can we have a biscuit now, both the same size?!!'

5   Michael is aged 5. According to Piaget, what stage of cognitive development would he be in?

☐   sensori-motor stage

☐   latent learning stage

☐   pre-operational stage

☐   genital stage

[1]

6   Why did Michael think that he had more drink than Patrick?

[2]

7   What did Piaget mean by the term *conservation*?

[2]

8   Source B is similar to the way that Piaget tested for conservation of volume. Describe **one** other way that Piaget tested for conservation in children.

[3]

9   Describe **two** criticisms of Piaget's work.

_____

_____

_____

_____

[4]

Chapter quiz

Answer the following questions in no longer than 10 minutes:

1   What was the basic method used by Piaget to study children's thinking?

2   What were the cognitive structures used for mental representation and thinking in Piaget's theory?

3   What name is given to the process of developing mental structures by incorporating new information without changing them?

4   In the young infant, what lack indicates the degree of the child's egocentricity?

5   Which term is missing from the following list: sensori-motor, concrete operational, formal operational?

6   Who used a naughty teddy to study conservation?

7   What did Hughes use to study egocentricity and decentering?

8   What game did Piaget use to study children's moral thinking?

9   If the young child is in a heteronomous stage of moral development, what stage is the older child in?

10   What was Kohlberg's second stage of moral development?

Appendix 1 – Ethical considerations

Ethics in psychological research – guidelines for students at pre-degree levels

Graham Davies, Geoff Haworth and Sue Hirschler
Standing Committee on Ethical Issues in Psychological Research
Association for the Teaching of Psychology

Source: Association for the Teaching of Psychology,
ATP Publications 1992

Aim

The aim of this document is to give guidelines to students involved in behavioural research in schools and colleges. It addresses many of the major issues, but does not cover all of them. Whilst the following guidelines refer to behavioural research in general, they are written specifically with psychological research in mind (for additional guidance see Further References, p200).

Introduction

Ethical issues arise whenever psychological research is carried out and you will need to consider these. Psychological investigations may have ethical implications for those participating in the study, others they have contact with, members of the public, the researcher and the reputation of psychology. You need to consider the rights and welfare of the people involved, the value of the knowledge obtained and the need to promote and maintain a positive image of psychology. Psychological research can be fun, but it should not be carried out just for fun.

If you ask people to help you with your research, they have the right to refuse. Respect their rights at all times and avoid exploiting them for your own interests.

Here are some of the questions you will need to ask yourself about any study you carry out:

- Should I be conducting this kind of study at all?
- What is the most ethical way of carrying it out?
- Am I sufficiently competent to carry it out?
- Have I informed the participants of all that they need and would expect to know before taking part?
- Have they willingly agreed to take part?
- How do I ensure that all research records are confidential and anonymous, and will remain so?
- How do I ensure that my research is carried out professionally and in a way that protects the rights of those involved?

Choosing the best method of study

However interesting your idea might seem, you should only proceed if your study can be ethically justified. You should familiarise yourself with previous relevant research and findings, and you should consult someone who is suitably experienced. The first person to approach will probably be a psychology teacher or lecturer.

If your research involves any of the following, you should discuss it with someone competent to advise you:

- psychological or physical discomfort
- invasion of privacy
- deception about the nature of the study or the participants' role in it

Competence

You need to work within your own limits, and seek advice from your teacher or lecturer in order to establish your competence level.

People may ask your advice because they know you are studying psychology. They may want help with personal problems which may be beyond your level of competence. Be very careful how you respond and do not claim to be more skilled or better qualified than you really are.

Consent

Unless you are observing public behaviour, participants should be volunteers and told what your research is about. Whenever possible, obtain their informed consent, making sure participants fully understand what they are agreeing to.

You will need to emphasise rather than cover up aspects of the study that might affect someone's willingness to help. It is unethical to deceive people into taking part by saying the study is about something else. You should only withhold information if the research cannot be carried out in any other way.

Participants should be debriefed so they know exactly what the study was about – be prepared to answer any questions. Their own results should be made available to them. If participants will be distressed or annoyed when you give them feedback at the end of the study, you should not proceed.

Participants have the right to withdraw from your study at any time – make sure they realise they can do this. Be prepared to stop the study immediately if you sense discomfort.

Participants should not be intimidated or pressurised into continuing when they do not want to, however inconvenient it is for you. You should be aware that participants may see you as threatening or in a position of influence simply because you are undertaking research.

Some people may be unable to give their own informed consent. These may include children, the elderly and those with special needs.

Research with children presents particular problems. Normally, you will need consent from a parent, guardian or from a person responsible for the child at the time of your study. For research conducted in a school, you should first obtain consent from the headteacher – this consent may also be required from parents or guardians. The headteacher will be able to advise you on this. In all circumstances, you must decide whether consent should be obtained from the child, and do this whenever possible.

Consent is not needed when carrying out naturalistic observations of behaviour in public places, but people's privacy should be respected. If you are researching on private property, such as a shopping precinct, it is a good idea to ask permission from the appropriate authorities. It is always best to check whether consent is required. Be aware that others may regard your behaviour as suspicious.

Confidentiality

Respect your participants' privacy by treating data as confidential. Others should be unable to identify those who have taken part in your study. Many researchers assign numbers or initials to participants, both to identify them in their reports and to maintain their anonymity. You may need to discuss your data with other researchers or your supervisor, so let participants know if you intend to do this. It is unethical to divulge individual data unless a participant has provided written permission for you to do so. Records should be kept safely and not left where others can gain access to them.

Conduct

You should always be honest about your own competence and limitations. You are unlikely to be an expert in diagnosis, psychotherapy or psychological testing. It is unethical to claim that you are.

Make sure you consider the welfare of those affected by your study. Maintain the highest standards of safety, ensuring that apparatus is safe and that participants do not attempt embarrassing, dangerous, painful or illegal tasks. Your study must be designed so that those involved are not exposed to physical or psychological risks at any time. If in doubt, discuss this with your psychology teacher or lecturer, and, if necessary, be prepared to abandon your study.

You should never:

- insult, offend or anger participants
- make participants believe that they have harmed or upset someone else
- break the law or encourage others to do so
- contravene the Data Protection Act
- illegally copy tests or materials
- make up data
- copy other people's work
- claim that somebody else's wording is your own

Research with non-human animals

Research with non-human animals presents additional problems and experimentation can rarely be justified at this level. Naturalistic research poses fewer problems, but field observations still need careful consideration. Animals may be disturbed and the breeding or survival of individuals, or of a whole species, may be threatened. Never cause animals more than minimal disturbance and avoid setting up any situation that causes them distress.

You should *only* conduct non-human animal research if:

- the investigation is planned in consultation with your psychology teacher or lecturer, and it is conducted with respect for animal life. *No* study should involve deprivation, distress or inflicting pain. Many forms of animal research are illegal unless you hold an appropriate Home Office licence
- you are sufficiently trained in the care and handling of any species involved, and you can ensure that the animals' needs are met. This means providing food and water and ensuring good housing, exercise, gentle handling and protection from disturbance by others.

Some examination boards will not allow you to submit research carried out on non-human animals.

Further references

American Psychological Association. 1983. *Ethical guidelines for the teaching of psychology in the secondary school*. Washington: APA

Bateson, P. 1986. 'When to experiment on animals'. *New Scientist*, 1496, pp 30–2

British Psychological Society. Scientific Affairs Board. 1985. "Guidelines for the use of animals in research". *Bulletin of the British Psychological Society*, 38. pp 289–91

British Psychological Society. 1978. 'Ethical principles for research with human subjects'. *Bulletin of the British Psychological Society,* 31. pp 48–9

British Psychological Society. 1985. 'A code of conduct for psychologists'. *Bulletin of the British Psychological Society*, 38. pp 41–3

British Psychological Society. 1990. 'Revised ethical principles'. *The Psychologist*, 3. pp 269–72

Vines, G. 1986. 'Experiments on animals: a balance of interests'. *New Scientist*, 1505. pp 26–7

Wadeley, A. 1991. *Ethics in psychological research and practice*, Leicester: British Psychological Society.

The address of The British Psychological society is:
St. Andrew's House, 48 Princess Road East, Leicester LE1 7DR

Ethical principles for conducting research with human participants

1 Introduction

1.1   The principles given below are intended to apply to research with human participants. Principles of conduct in professional practice are to be found in the Society's Code of Conduct and in the advisory documents prepared by the Divisions, Sections and Special Groups of the Society.

1.2   Participants in psychological research should have confidence in the investigators. Good psychological research is possible only if there is mutual respect and confidence between investigators and participants. Psychological investigators are potentially interested in all aspects of human behaviour and conscious experience. However, for ethical reasons, some areas of human experience and behaviour may be beyond the reach of experiment, observation or other form of psychological investigation. Ethical guidelines are necessary to clarify the conditions under which psychological research is acceptable.

1.3   The principles given below supplement for researchers with human participants the general ethical principles of members of the Society as stated in the British Psychological Society's Code of Conduct (1985). Members of the British Psychological Society are expected to abide by both the Code of Conduct and the fuller principles expressed here. Members should also draw the principles to the attention of research colleagues who are not members of the Society. Members should encourage colleagues to adopt them and ensure that they are followed by all researchers whom they supervise (e.g. research assistants, postgraduate, undergraduate, A-Level and GCSE students).

1.4   In recent years, there has been an increase in legal actions by members of the general public against professionals for alleged misconduct. Researchers must recognise the possibility of such legal action if they infringe the rights and dignity of participants in their research.

2 General

2.1   In all circumstances, investigators must consider the ethical implications and psychological consequences for the participants in their research. The essential principle is that the investigation should be considered from the standpoint of all participants; foreseeable threats to their psychological well-being, health, values or dignity should be eliminated. Investigators should recognise that, in our multi-cultural and multi-ethnic society and where investigations involve individuals of different ages, gender and social background, the investigators may not have sufficient knowledge of the implications of an investigation for the participants. It should be borne in mind that the best judges of whether an investigation will cause offence may be members of the population from which the participants in the research are to be drawn.

3 Consent

3.1   Whenever possible, the investigator should inform all participants of the objectives of the investigation. The investigator should inform the participants of all aspects of the research or intervention that might reasonably be expected to influence willingness to participate. The investigator should, normally, explain all other aspects of the research or intervention about which the participants enquire. Failure to make full disclosure prior to obtaining informed consent requires additional safeguards to protect the welfare and dignity of the participants (see Section 4).

3.2   Research with children or with participants who have impairments that will limit understanding and/or communication such that they are unable to give their real consent requires special safeguarding procedures.

3.3   Where possible, the real consent of children and of adults with impairments in understanding or communication should be obtained. In addition, where research involves all persons under sixteen years of age, consent should be obtained from parents or from those *in loco parentis*.

3.4   Where real consent cannot be obtained from adults with impairments in understanding or communication, wherever possible the investigator should consult a person well-placed to appreciate the participant's reaction, such as a member of the person's family, and must obtain the disinterested approval of the research from independent advisors.

3.5   When research is being conducted with detained persons, particular care should be taken over informed consent, paying attention to the special circumstances which may affect the person's ability to give free informed consent.

3.6   Investigators should realise that they are often in a position of authority or influence over participants who may be their students, employees or clients. This relationship must not be allowed to pressurise the participants to take part in, or remain in, an investigation.

3.7   The payment of participants must not be used to induce them to risk harm beyond that which they risk without payment in their normal lifestyle.

3.8   If harm, unusual discomfort, or other negative consequences for the individual's future life might occur, the investigator must obtain the disinterested approval of independent advisors, inform the participants, and obtain informed, real consent from each of them.

3.9   In longitudinal research, consent may need to be obtained on more than one occasion.

4 Deception

4.1   The withholding of information or the misleading of participants is unacceptable if the participants are typically likely to object or show unease once debriefed. Where this is in any doubt, appropriate consultation must precede the investigation. Consultation is best carried out with individuals who share the social and cultural background of the participants in the research, but the advice of ethics committees or experienced and disinterested colleagues may be sufficient.

4.2   Intentional deception of the participants over the purpose and general nature of the investigation should be avoided whenever possible. Participants should never be deliberately misled without extremely strong scientific or medical justification. Even then there should be strict controls and the disinterested approval of independent advisors.

4.3   It may be impossible to study some psychological processes without withholding information about the true object of the study or deliberately misleading the participants. Before conducting such a study, the investigator has a special responsibility to (a) determine that alternative procedures avoiding concealment or deception are not available, (b) ensure that the participants are provided with sufficient information at the earliest stage; and (c) consult appropriately upon the way that the withholding of information or deliberate deception will be received

5 Debriefing

5.1   In studies where the participants are aware that they have taken part in an investigation, when the data have been collected, the investigator should provide the participants with any necessary information to complete their understanding of the nature of the research. The investigator should discuss with the participants their experience of the research in order to monitor any unforeseen negative effects or misconceptions.

5.2   Debriefing does not provide a justification for unethical aspects of an investigation.

5.3   Some effects which may be produced by an experiment will not be negated by a verbal description following the research. Investigators have a responsibility to ensure that participants receive any necessary debriefing in the form of active intervention before they leave the research setting.

6 Withdrawal from the investigation

6.1   At the onset of the investigation investigators should make plain to participants their right to withdraw from the research at any time, irrespective of whether or not payment or other inducement has been offered. It is recognised that this may be difficult in certain observational or organisational settings, but nevertheless the investigator must attempt to ensure that participants (including children) know of their right to withdraw. When testing children, avoidance of the testing situation may be taken as evidence of failure to consent to the procedure and should be acknowledged.

6.2   In the light of experience of the investigation, or as a result of debriefing, the participant has the right to withdraw retrospectively any consent given, and to require that their own data, including recordings, be destroyed.

7 Confidentiality

7.1   Subject to the requirements of legislation, including the Data Protection Act, information obtained about a participant during an investigation is confidential unless otherwise agreed in advance. Investigators who are put under pressure to disclose confidential information should draw this point to the attention of those exerting such pressure. Participants in psychological research have a right to expect that information they provide will be treated confidentially and, if published, will not be identifiable as theirs. In the event that confidentiality and/or anonymity cannot be guaranteed, the participant must be warned of this in advance of agreeing to participate.

8 Protection of participants

8.1   Investigators have a primary responsibility to protect participants from physical and mental harm during the investigation. Normally, the risk of harm must be no greater than in ordinary life, i.e. participants should not be exposed to risks greater than or additional to those encountered in their normal lifestyles. Where the risk of harm is greater than in ordinary life the provisions of 3.8 should apply. Participants must be asked about any factors in the procedure that might create a risk, such as pre-existing medical conditions, and must be advised of any special action they should take to avoid risk.

8.2   Participants should be informed of procedures for contacting the investigator within a reasonable time period following participation should stress, potential harm, or related questions or concern arise despite the precautions required by these Principles. Where research procedures might result in undesirable consequences for participants, the investigator has the responsibility to detect and remove or correct these consequences.

8.3   Where research may involve behaviour or experiences that participants may regard as personal and private the participants must be protected from stress by all appropriate measures, including the assurance that answers to personal questions need not be given. There should be no concealment or deception when seeking information that might encroach on privacy.

8.4   In research involving children, great caution should be exercised when discussing the results with parents, teachers or others *in loco parentis*, since evaluative statements may carry unintended weight.

9 Observational research

9.1   Studies based upon observation must respect the privacy and psychological well-being of the individuals studied. Unless those observed give their consent to being observed, observational research is only acceptable in situations where those observed would expect to be observed by strangers. Additionally, particular account should be taken of local cultural values and of the possibility of intruding upon the privacy of individuals who, even while in a normally public space, may believe they are unobserved.

10 Giving advice

10.1   During research, an investigator may obtain evidence of psychological or physical problems of which a participant is, apparently, unaware. In such a case, the investigator has a responsibility to inform the participant if the investigator believes that by not doing so the participant's future well being may be endangered.

10.2   If, in the normal course of psychological research, or as a result of problems detected as in 10.1, a participant solicits advice concerning educational, personality, behavioural or health issues, caution should be exercised. If the issue is serious and the investigator is not qualified to offer assistance, the appropriate source of professional advice should be recommended. Further details on the giving of advice will be found in the Society's Code of Conduct.

10.3   In some kinds of investigation the giving of advice is appropriate if this forms an intrinsic part of the research and has been agreed in advance.

11 Colleagues

11.1   Investigators share responsibility for the ethical treatment of research participants with their collaborators, assistants, students and employees. A psychologist who believes that another psychologist or investigator may be conducting research that is not in accordance with the principles above should encourage that investigator to re-evaluate the research.

Source: British Psychological Society, *The Psychologist*, vol.3, no. 6, June 1990

Appendix 2 – Illustrating the results of practicals

A: Tables

A table is a chart, divided into columns (pointing downwards) and rows (pointing across). This makes a series of squares in the centre of the table.

The simplest type of table is 2×2, which means that it has two columns and two rows, making four squares (or 'cells') altogether. But a table can have as many rows or columns as it needs.

Traditionally, the rows say things about your research participants, so if you were looking at, say, older and younger people, the top row would be scores from younger people and the bottom one would be scores from older people.

The columns indicate other things about your data. If you are giving the mean, mode and median, for instance, these would form the three columns of your table. If your data are divided into other categories, such as types of behaviour or responses to different parts of a test, then these should be the columns.

To draw up a table, first work out how many columns you are going to need, and how many rows. Then draw up a grid showing these. Remember to label each row and each column, and remember also to give your table a general title which describes what it is about.

When you have drawn up your grid, look at each cell in turn and write in the score that belongs to it. You can work this out by looking upwards to see which column it is in, and along to see which row it is in. For instance, a cell that was in the 'mean' column and in the 'younger participants' row would need to have the mean score from the younger group written in it. (That's why it's so important to label each column and row – so that you can work out what goes into the cells more easily!)

When you have entered something in each of the cells of your grid, your table has been completed.

Column labels

	Mean	Mode	Median
Younger participants	4.7	6	5
Older participants	4.4	5	4.5

Row labels

Cells

This table summarises the following set of data:

Younger participants: 5, 6, 2, 3, 3, 7, 6, 4, 6, 5
Older participants: 4, 3, 3, 7, 4, 5, 2, 5, 6, 5

B: Bar charts

A bar chart is a way of saying how much, or how many, you have of each category, or type, of score.

In a bar chart, the bottom line (which is called the horizontal axis) is divided into sections. Each section represents a particular type of score. For instance, if you had collected data about favourite colours, each section on the horizontal axis of your bar chart would represent a different colour.

The line which runs up the left-hand side of your bar chart is known as the vertical axis. It is used for counting the number of scores that you have in each category, so it needs to be divided up evenly, and the highest number on that line should be just above the highest number of scores in your data.

To draw up a bar chart: first, put your data into categories, or types, and count how many you have in each one.

Divide the bottom line into sections, one for each category. Label the sections (for example, 'yellow', 'green', 'blue', etc.), and put in a general label for the bottom line as well (such as 'colours').

Look at your data and see which category has the highest number of scores in it. Make this number, or the round number just above it, the top of your vertical axis. Divide the rest of the vertical axis evenly, from 0 upwards, and number them. (You may want to divide it using groups of 5, 10 or 20 instead of numbering each point on the scale.) Put in a general label for the vertical axis as well (for example, 'number of answers').

Now take your first set of scores, see how many there are in the category and draw a rectangle on your bar chart. The base of the rectangle should fit into the section of the bottom line which you have given to that category. The height of the rectangle should correspond to the point where that number would come on the vertical axis if you were to move it across into that section.

Colour that bar in, or shade it with stripes, and then draw the next bar, using your second set of scores. Carry on doing this until a rectangle has been drawn for each category.

You have now drawn a bar chart.

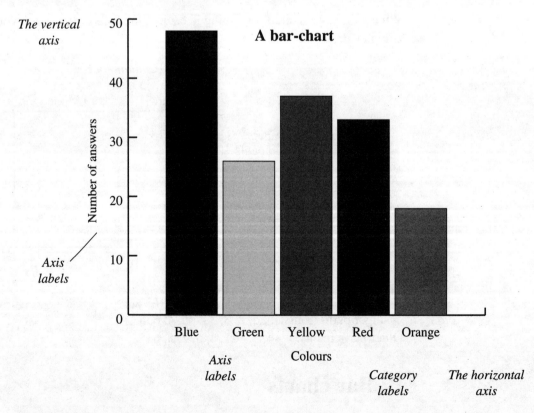

This bar-chart summarises the following set of scores:
blue = 48, green = 26, yellow = 37, red = 33, orange = 18

C: Graphs

A graph is a way of showing how a particular score has changed under different circumstances.

In a graph, the bottom line (which is called the horizontal axis) is always a continuous scale, such as time, amount or distance. It is divided into sections for convenience, and the divisions allow you to know when a measurement took place. In a temperature graph, for instance, the bottom line indicates times during the course of a day.

The line which runs up the left-hand side of your graph is known as the vertical axis. It is used for indicating how high or low a score is at the point when it was measured. For this reason, it needs to be evenly divided up, and the highest number on that line should be just above the highest number of scores in your data. On a temperature graph, it would be just above the highest temperature that you have measured.

To draw up a graph, first draw and label the horizontal axis and the vertical axis. The furthest point on the horizontal axis represents the highest, most recent or most extreme point at which you took a measurement.

Look at your scores, and put an × on the chart to represent each score. The height of the × says how large the score is, and the distance across the chart says when the score was taken.

When you have plotted all of the scores in this way, join them all up with as smooth a line as possible.

You have now drawn a graph.

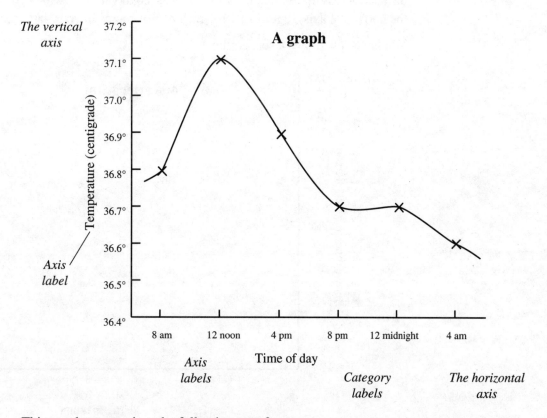

This graph summarises the following set of scores:
8 am = 36.8°, 12 noon = 37.1°, 4 pm = 36.9°, 8 pm = 36.7°, 12 midnight = 36.7°, 4 am = 36.6°

D: Scattergrams

A scattergram is a way of showing how closely different pairs of scores resemble one another. It is only used to illustrate correlations.

A scattergram consists of a series of points, usually put in as ×s, which are drawn in the space between the horizontal and the vertical axis.

Each point represents a score which is formed from a measure of the first variable (represented by the horizontal axis) and the second variable (represented by the vertical axis). So, in a scattergram, each axis represents a different kind of variable or measurement.

Each variable in a correlation is a continuous scale, such as time, amount or distance. For this reason, each axis is divided into sections for convenience, and the divisions allow you to know what the value of that variable was when each measurement took place.

In a scattergram comparing temperature and alertness, for instance, the temperature axis (which could be either the vertical or the horizontal one) indicates what the person's temperature was when it was measured, while the alertness axis gives a measure of how alert they felt.

To draw up a scattergram, first draw and label the horizontal axis and the vertical axis. They should be of equal length. The furthest point on each axis should be just beyond the highest, most recent or most extreme value of that type of measurement.

Look at your scores and put an × on the chart to represent each score. The height of the × is the value of the first variable (which you have shown on the vertical axis), and the distance across the chart is the value of the second variable (which you have shown on the horizontal axis). Put in an × for each pair of scores in your data.

You have now drawn a scattergram.

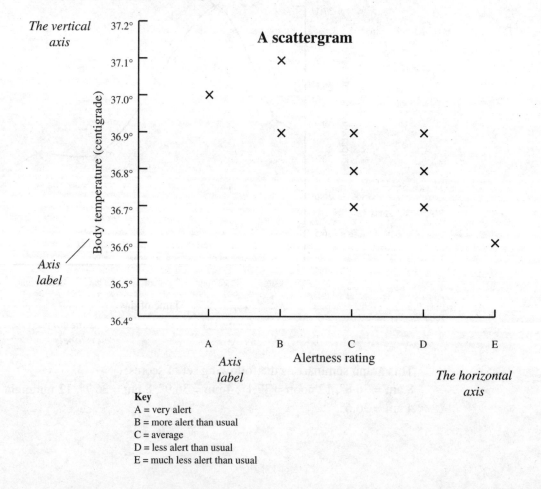

The vertical axis

A scattergram

Body temperature (centigrade)

37.2°
37.1°
37.0°
36.9°
36.8°
36.7°
36.6°
36.5°
36.4°

Axis label

A   B   C   D   E

Alertness rating

Axis label

The horizontal axis

Key
A = very alert
B = more alert than usual
C = average
D = less alert than usual
E = much less alert than usual

This scattergram summarises the following set of scores

B + 37.1°   C + 36.9°   D + 36.7°   D + 36.9°   B = 36.9°

D + 36.8°   C + 36.7°   E + 36.6°   A + 37°   C = 36.8°

Checklist A: Experimental studies

- [ ] TITLE

- [ ] ABSTRACT
- [ ] area covered
- [ ] what you did
- [ ] what you found
- [ ] conclusion

- [ ] INTRODUCTION
- [ ] general introduction
- [ ] relevant studies
- [ ] introduction to this study
- [ ] aims of study
- [ ] hypothesis
- [ ] null hypothesis

- [ ] METHOD
- [ ] design used
- [ ] independent and dependent variables
- [ ] type of data collected
- [ ] the number of research participants in each condition, and the total
- [ ] age range/gender of research participants in each condition
- [ ] sampling method used
- [ ] the materials used
- [ ] the appendix in which the materials may be found
- [ ] details of any controls used
- [ ] exactly what you did
- [ ] the instructions you gave
- [ ] the way you analysed the results

- [ ] RESULTS
- [ ] Table 1 (as described in Appendix 2)
- [ ] Figure 1 (as described in Appendix 2)
- [ ] a brief description of the results in words

- [ ] DISCUSSION
- [ ] whether the results support the hypothesis
- [ ] problems with the study
- [ ] suggested improvements to the study
- [ ] how the results relate to other psychological work
- [ ] possible further studies

- [ ] APPENDIX
- [ ] materials used in the study (such as score sheets)
- [ ] raw data obtained from research participants
- [ ] calculations for means etc.

Checklist B: Correlational studies

- [ ] TITLE

- [ ] ABSTRACT
- [ ] area covered
- [ ] what you did
- [ ] what you found
- [ ] conclusion

- [ ] INTRODUCTION
- [ ] general introduction
- [ ] relevant studies
- [ ] introduction to this study
- [ ] aims of the study
- [ ] aims of study
- [ ] hypothesis
- [ ] null hypothesis

- [ ] METHOD
- [ ] state that it was a correlation
- [ ] type of data collected
- [ ] variables to be correlated
- [ ] details of any controls used
- [ ] the number of research participants
- [ ] how many males and females
- [ ] age range of participants
- [ ] sampling method used
- [ ] the materials used
- [ ] the appendix in which the materials may be found
- [ ] exactly what you did
- [ ] the instructions you gave
- [ ] the way you analysed the results

- [ ] RESULTS
- [ ] Figure 1 (a scattergram)
- [ ] a brief description of the results in words

- [ ] DISCUSSION
- [ ] whether the results support the hypothesis
- [ ] problems with the study
- [ ] suggested improvements to the study
- [ ] how the results relate to other psychological work
- [ ] possible further studies

- [ ] APPENDIX
- [ ] materials used in the study (such as score sheets)
- [ ] raw data from research participants

Checklist C: Observational studies

- ☐ TITLE

- ☐ ABSTRACT
- ☐ area covered
- ☐ what you did
- ☐ what you found
- ☐ conclusion

- ☐ INTRODUCTION
- ☐ general introduction
- ☐ relevant studies
- ☐ introduction to this study
- ☐ aims of the study
- ☐ aims of study
- ☐ hypothesis (if you used one)
- ☐ null hypothesis (if you used one)

- ☐ METHOD
- ☐ type of observation used
- ☐ type of data collected
- ☐ details of any controls used
- ☐ the number of research participants
- ☐ how many males and females
- ☐ age range of participants
- ☐ sampling method used
- ☐ details about observer(s) age,sex, etc.
- ☐ the materials used
- ☐ the appendix in which the materials may be found
- ☐ exactly what you did
- ☐ the instructions you gave
- ☐ the way you analysed the results

- ☐ RESULTS
- ☐ Table 1 (as described)
- ☐ Figure 1 (bar charts are usually used for this type of data)
- ☐ a brief description of the results in words

- ☐ DISCUSSION
- ☐ whether the results support the hypothesis or the aims
- ☐ problems with the study
- ☐ suggested improvements to the study
- ☐ how the results relate to other psychological work
- ☐ possible further studies

- ☐ APPENDIX
- ☐ materials used in the study (such as score sheets)
- ☐ raw data from research participants

Checklist D: Test and questionnaire development

- ☐ TITLE

- ☐ ABSTRACT
- ☐ area covered
- ☐ what you did
- ☐ what the result was like

- ☐ INTRODUCTION
- ☐ general introduction
- ☐ relevant studies
- ☐ introduction to this study
- ☐ aims of the study

- ☐ METHOD
- ☐ type of data collected
- ☐ details of any precautions or controls used
- ☐ the number of research participants
- ☐ how many males and females
- ☐ age range of participants
- ☐ sampling method used
- ☐ details about data collector(s) age, sex, etc.
- ☐ exactly what you did
- ☐ the instructions you gave
- ☐ the way you collected the results
- ☐ how the data was organised into a test
- ☐ how the test was evaluated
- ☐ the appendix in which the materials may be found

- ☐ RESULTS
- ☐ the test itself
- ☐ the outcome of a simple pilot of the test
- ☐ Figure 1 (bar charts are usually used for this type of data)
- ☐ a brief description of the results in words

- ☐ DISCUSSION
- ☐ whether the test assesses what it is supposed to
- ☐ problems with the test
- ☐ suggested improvements to the test
- ☐ ways of assessing validity, reliability, etc.
- ☐ possible further applications of the test

- ☐ APPENDIX
- ☐ materials used in the study (such as score sheets)
- ☐ raw data from research participants during the pilot

Appendix 4 – Answers to chapter quizzes

Chapter 1

1　23
2　recessive
3　an egg
4　they are precocial
5　it is red
6　they are clones
7　learning/environment
8　a critical period
9　genetic engineering
10　stereotyped

Chapter 2

1　the generalisation gradient
2　vasoconstriction
3　cranberry jelly
4　trace conditioning
5　the Law of Effect
6　fixed-interval
7　primary reinforcement
8　insight learning
9　rhesus monkeys
10　cognitive maps

Chapter 3

1　mental age
2　eugenics
3　Cyril Burt
4　monozygotic
5　schizophrenia
6　R. D. Laing
7　appeasement gestures
8　the frustration-aggression hypothesis
9　Calhoun
10　empiricist

Chapter 4

1　Kohler
2　the kitten carousel
3　the Cree indians
4　Gibson and Walk
5　pattern perception
6　colour constancy
7　binocular depth cues
8　dogs
9　the visual cortex
10　peek-a-boo

Chapter 5

1　spinal cord
2　connector
3　neurotransmitter
4　absolute refractory period
5　the myelin sheath
6　acetylcholine
7　corpus callosum
8　sub-cortical structures
9　loudness and pitch (or intensity and frequency)
10　transduction

Chapter 6

1　the pilomotor response
2　the general adaptation syndrome
3　lie-detector
4　the sympathetic division
5　Levine
6　rats
7　the Yerkes-Dodson Law
8　implosion therapy
9　Ax
10　the social situation

Chapter 7

1　paradoxical
2　physiological correlates of sleep
3　circadian
4　jet lag
5　cats
6　lucid dreams
7　dreamwork
8　hallucinogens
9　alpha rhythms
10　a sedative

Chapter 8

1　Korsakoff's syndrome
2　simple, complex and hypercomplex cells
3　sensory projection areas
4　Wilder Penfield
5　Wernicke's area
6　lesion
7　hemispherectomy
8　equipotentiality
9　scanning
10　epilepsy

Chapter 9

1 Dewey
2 incubation
3 puzzle box
4 the Aha! experience
5 lateral thinking
6 functional fixedness
7 protocols
8 Locke
9 computer simulation
10 time taken to agree/disagree

Chapter 10

1 linguistic relativity
2 egocentricity
3 the expressive function
4 elaborated code
5 semantic relations grammar
6 phonemes
7 Language Acquisition Device
8 social experience
9 phylogenetic scale
10 gorilla

Chapter 11

1 Loftus and Loftus
2 effort after meaning
3 serial reproduction
4 anterograde amnesia
5 repression
6 state-dependent learning
7 enactive, iconic and symbolic
8 levels of processing
9 new radio frequencies
10 method of loci

Chapter 12

1 the Gestalt psychologists
2 figure/ground organisation
3 the principle of closure
4 motivation
5 subliminal perception
6 Broadbent
7 shadowing
8 Triesman
9 semantic processing
10 anticipatory schemata

Chapter 13

1 nomothetic
2 id, ego, superego
3 projection
4 libido
5 neuroticism
6 RAS. (reticular activating system)
7 life-data
8 need for self-actualisation
9 Q-sort
10 personal constructs

Chapter 14

1 nomothetic
2 the normal distribution curve
3 standardisation
4 Terman
5 deviation IQ
6 general intelligence
7 seven
8 contextual, experience and componential
9 job aptitude and ability tests
10 aptitude tests

Chapter 15

1 homeostasis
2 VMH (ventro-medial hypothalamus)
3 rats
4 Schachter
5 electrical stimulation of the brain
6 cognitive dissonance
7 approach-avoidance
8 internal locus of control
9 social representations
10 social respect

Chapter 16

1 central traits
2 halo effects
3 primacy effects
4 Lloyd
5 fundamental attribution error
6 consistency, consensus and distinctiveness
7 Newcomb
8 a computer dance
9 cognitive, affective and behavioural (or conative)
10 Sherif

Chapter 17

1   verbal communication
2   it is symbolic
3   paralanguage
4   Kendon
5   pupil dilation
6   the eyebrow flash
7   facial electromyography
8   Hall
9   illustrators and regulators
10 cross-cultural, laboratory and comparative studies

Chapter 18

1   sanctions
2   50%
3   nurses
4   Perrin and Spencer
5   imitation
6   75%
7   diffusion of responsibility
8   Tajfel and Turner
9   social representations
10 Hindu and Muslim

Chapter 19

1   smiling
2   baby-talk
3   Jaffe
4   a blind baby
5   the Moro reflex
6   imitation
7   a Bobo doll
8   physical and psychological punishment
9   Kessen
10 the grandparents

Chapter 20

1   anal and phallic
2   anal retentiveness
3   the phallic stage
4   castration threat anxiety
5   Little Hans
6   ego-defence mechanisms
7   adolescence
8   generativity/stagnation
9   Clarke and Clarke
10 imprinting

Chapter 21

1   clinical interviews
2   schemas (or schemata)
3   assimilation
4   object constancy
5   pre-operational
6   McGarrigle
7   policeman and boy dolls
8   marbles
9   autonomous
10 conventional morality